Thank you + looking after

Pat and Murel Callis

Life is what you make it!
Book II

by

Muriel & Pat Callis

River Rafting, Jasper Canada

Our final book is dedicated to the founders of the charities we support, Pam Young (Mali), Wendy Valentine (Animal Sanctuary), whom we hold in high esteem, for their courage, bravery, determination and tenacity in the work they undertake.

There are so many friends that we owe our gratitude to, some have been mentioned in the book. We are particularly grateful to Martin Fox and Sheila Reynolds who helped with the proof reading, also our friend Val, in Dore for her help and encouragement when we were writing about our last years in Sheffield. Lastly to our publishers for their friendship and patience.

To our readers we hope our books will give you as much pleasure as it has given us writing them.

First published in Great Britain in 2017 by RMC Media
RMC Media – www.rmcmedia.co.uk/books
6 Broadfield Court, Sheffield, S8 0XF
Tel: 0114 250 6300

Editor: Chris Brierley
Design: Dan Wray

Printed and bound in Great Britain by CPI Colour Ltd.

A CIP catalogue record for this book is available from the British Library.

ISBN: 978-1-907998-33-1

Contents

Part III
Challenges, Trials, Happiness and Sadness
Page 7

Part IV
Decisions to be Made
Page 49

Part V
Searching, Finding and Retiring
Page 73

Part VI
Village Life
Page 143

Challenges, Trials, Happiness and Sadness

We continue our story in the middle 60's and open with Muriel being without a job following the death of her boss.

My first port of call was a visit to the Labour Exchange to register myself as unemployed!

At my interview, I stressed that I hoped it would not be too long before I found suitable employment in my profession. Imagine my surprise at the end of the interview I was asked to wait to see the person in charge, who offered me a position in their office as I was mature and used to meeting people! I explained to her that I wished to follow my career in Dentistry and was hopeful that I would hear soon of a suitable position. She accepted this, but the post was still available, if I changed my mind.

That same evening I had a telephone call from Mary, the local association secretary to tell me of a vacancy for a trained person at Woodseats. I made contact by telephone and went the following evening for an interview with the Dentist and the Associate from his branch practice at Bolsover in North Derbyshire. It was a good all round Practice undertaking most types of treatment, with one surgery at each place. The branch surgery was in dire need of a trained dental nurse, the previous one having been dismissed under strange circumstances. The Woodseats surgery required the books making up to date for the previous two years! I felt it would be a challenge! I asked about my Conditions of Employment.

1. To be on the salary scale as recommended by the Joint Committee of the British Dental Association and the Dental Nurses Association.

2. The provision of an Insurance Policy for Superannuation purposes.
3. That I was on the Committee of the Dental Nurses Association and occasionally would require a day off to attend meetings in London.

Both dentists were members of their Professional Organisation (BDA) so it was easy to say what I expected and it was all agreed.

I accepted the position offered and began my new challenge the following week.

It soon became obvious, with all the travelling, I would require a vehicle. We saw in the local paper an Austin 30 Van for Sale locally for £100. It was in quite good condition and saw me through the first winter. I subsequently sold it for £100, in part exchange for a new Fiat 125.

The accommodation at Woodseats was one surgery upstairs in the back room, a second room was the laboratory and there was a bathroom and toilet. Downstairs the hall had a room on the left which was the waiting room. At the end of the hall on the left there was a further room which was full of rubbish and papers. On the right there was a kitchen which served as an office. The Bolsover Branch was above a post office, one room was a surgery. There was a small room with the usual facilities and quite a large room for the waiting room. There were plans to expand the two premises at some stage, but my first priority was to create some semblance of order! I had a call from the Accountant asking me to provide him with some figures as soon as possible. With the help of bank statements and a book keeping book, things started to slot into position. It was a relief that my boss had a part time appointment at the Sheffield Dental Hospital and I was able to spend his two half days sorting these out. I also had to spend quite a lot of time at the Branch Practice, including two nights working in the surgery until 8pm.

Fortunately we soon found a trained Dental Nurse to work in Bolsover. It was an interesting area to be involved in, with many diverse patients, farmers, miners, including those working at the coal face, the office staff and the bosses, market gardeners, many came from the Polish Community and rented plots of land to farm. I found different routes to reach Bolsover. The Castle situated on the hill was the focal point to aim for, the town was quite flat terrain. The Boss soon found a plot of land and one of the patients was an architect, so the wheels were put into motion for a new purpose built Dental Surgery, a very exciting time.

Meanwhile at Woodseats we had finally cleared the back room. The office was moved into the kitchen after the builder had removed the old kitchen fire range and put a new lintel in to hold everything in place, making an alcove for the filing cabinets. A very messy and dusty time!

The office and back room which overlooked the garden were both decorated, the carpets cleaned and finally the furniture was moved into a new clean waiting room. At last there was an empty room at the front to make a second surgery, which would be a blessing for our elderly patients.

The boss wanted all the latest equipment and this required a trip to London! So the boss, a dental representative, and myself boarded the early morning Master Cutler train for our journey with breakfast served on board, to St. Pancras Station. The first call was to the showrooms to see the types of equipment that was required, then on to have lunch at Simpsons, in Piccadilly. This gave us the opportunity to discuss and decide which pieces of equipment to purchase before returning to the showroom to confirm the order. Business completed it was back home on the Master Cutler. All these changes happened in my first three years, proving to be a real challenge as we continued seeing patients throughout the alterations.

Towards the end of 1966, Muriel was invited to attend a special Ceremony at St John's Gate Clerkenwell, London. The Investiture took place early in 1967 and we were able to take one guest, so Mother came for a day out. We travelled on the 7.30am train to London. It was rather a sombre event with Lord Wakehurst presenting me, along with many other members, the Badge of Serving Sister, for giving over 20 years service to the Order of St. John. My memory of the day is a little sparse, but it was interesting to see inside the Headquarters. Mother enjoyed the day and coming home we were able to have a meal on the train.

Pat was also having a busy time! Following three months abroad, I had to write detailed reports on my experiences to the Scholarship Committee and to the Local Authority. I also gave several talks with slides. I was particularly keen to commence 'Preparation for Childbirth Classes', using the Psychoprophylactic method which I had witnessed in Paris.

Just before Christmas 1965, I had a telephone call, from a lady who was expecting her baby in February 1966. She had heard that I was starting some classes and she would like to attend! The first week in January an 8 week course commenced with a small group of pregnant ladies who came to our house in the evening. With very little equipment and in my own time we completed the first course. The word soon got round and I became a member of the National Childbirth Trust and commenced regular classes. Because

EASING THE PAIN OF CHILDBIRTH

CENTURIES of fear and ignorance, and a degree of genuinely painful experience, have conditioned most women into believing that their one function in childbirth is to suffer.

They have little knowledge of and no authority over the situation. The skill, pleasure and sense of achievement in a tough job well done belong to somebody else.

But in the last 18 months Preparation for Childbirth, but its proper name is psychoprophylaxis. The Russians started it in 1940 when, in order to encourage women to have more babies, doctors applied Pavlov's theory of conditioned reflexes to parturition.

After the last war the method spread to France, and now about half the women there are prepared for childbirth in this way. Recently, Miss Pat Callis, Sheffield's Assistant Supervisor of Midwives, found that in one Paris hospital 90.16 per cent... When one group of ...cles contract, it is ...nal for other muscles in ...he time. In labour, of ...rse, it is the uterus which ...tracts, and it is the asso-

home births and the other half hospital ones.

There is no shortage of requests from women wanting preparation (even those due to have their offspring in nursing homes), and a thick file of thank-you letters in Miss Callis's office is proof of its widely acknowledged...

When a woman gives birth to a baby, muscles other than those used in the delivery contract—and it is these that cause pain. A method of relaxing these other muscles, thus lessening pain, is being used increasingly in Sheffield. Pat Roberts reports . . .

ciated contraction of other muscle, which causes pain.

Through psychoprophylaxis, women can learn to relax these other muscles even at the height of uterine contractions.

They are taught this during pregnancy by simulating labour. They contract an arm and concentrate on relaxation elsewhere. Then a leg, then an arm and leg on the same side of the body, then an arm and leg on opposite sides (very difficult, this one).

Eventually, they become so expert that when labour day arrives, they know precisely... the ... method, so replacing the older type of relaxation class.

At the outset, most of the women who had this training had their babies at home. But now about half are

Miss ...they c ...cent. ...but inc ...underst ...laxis a ...wrong ...scious ...tions i

Miss ...musculi ...learning ...breathi ...ing g ...emphas ...You ...her else ...ing be ...produce ...magic. ...Much ...and she ...uterus ...to worl ...or baby ...normal, ...perfect ...called i ...prophy. ...mostly. ...was cause ...that he ...the sandw ...brought al

Tomor ...and

Pat Roberts ends her report

The moment of birth

THE now famous film "Birthday," made for the National Childbirth Trust on psychoprophylaxis, shows two mothers during delivery.

One smiles as she looks at, and touches and talks to, her half-born baby, hardly able to wait for the moment she can nurse him.

The other is actually having a good giggle—and enjoying it so much that it's difficult not to laugh with her.

All the women undergoing preparation for childbirth in the same way in Sheffield see the film, usually accompanied by their husbands.

But how typical of psychoprophylaxis are the two births on film, and how do they differ from ordinary births?

Since the Sheffield Maternity and Child Welfare service started teaching this system 20 months ago, several women having their second babies have followed the course and are now able to compare the new method with the old one by which they had their first babies.

Most of them are impressed during psychoprophylaxis classes to find that more time is devoted to preparation for

AND FOR TWO WOMEN IT'S SHEER DELIGHT

wasn't necessary. He is now converted.

Concentration, says Mrs. Rowntree, is vital to the success of psychoprophylaxis. Once you've got that you gain in confidence and are able to understand, co-operate and achieve so that labour can be very gratifying.

"I'm expecting my third baby in a few weeks' time and am actually looking forward to a marvellous experience."

Mrs. Enid Elliott, of Hale Street, Sheffield, had her first baby, Sean, in hospital.

"Explanations in the talks I attended were helpful, but when I went to psychoprophylaxis classes for my second baby the explanations were even better.

BOOK

"This time I knew exactly when to go into hospital. With the first baby I was anxiously noting the time between contractions."

Mrs. Elliott attended sessions at Broadfield Road clinic. She says the course of the large classes I booked a room in the Local Memorial Rooms. Husbands were encouraged to come to the classes and the mothers, after delivery, were asked to write about their experience.

The classes were then transferred to the Health Education Centre. The numbers waiting to attend them grew much larger to the point of difficulties in accommodating over 40 ladies plus husbands. I had to organise a method of encompassing every body. This was for half the class to arrive to do the exercises, after which the other half arrived to attend together for the talk and question time. The first half left and the second half completed the session with their exercises. In 1967 Pat Roberts a journalist came to a course of classes and wrote a very full account for the local newspaper. More classes were started and courses for midwives and student midwives to learn the technique.

Although one can not promise a hundred per cent success and labours do vary, from the many letters I received it showed the majority had benefited from understanding more about labour and by following the two basic principles of muscular disassociation combined with a breathing pattern, together with the support of their partners.

I still practice the principles of the technique when having dental treatment without the need for a local anaesthetic.

In the late 60's changes occurred with more mothers being delivered in hospital which meant the District Midwives were having less home deliveries, but a larger caseload of early discharges from hospital. The Midwives working on the wards were used to having post natal mothers in hospital for up to 10 days, with many now going home as early as 48 hours caused some unrest among the Midwives. I felt I should have a change and in 1968 a Tutors post at Northern General Hospital was advertised in the Nursing Press, I applied and was accepted. I still continued taking classes in my own time for the National Childbirth Trust.

Returning to family events, in May 1966 we had a holiday on the Isle of

Spud bashing!

Wight. We went to Lymington by car boarding the ferry to take us to Yarmouth, from there we drove to Totland, where we stayed in a very nice hotel. Also staying in the same Hotel was a well known actor and actress with their little boy called Jason, the actor had been 'Dr Who' at some stage, it rings a bell that the lady was Joan Greenwood. We can still remember hearing them calling 'Jason' a rather precocious little boy who loved having Pat reading stories to him!

We were able to visit Carrisbrooke Castle and watch the donkeys turning the wheel to bring up the water from the well. Osborne House and gardens, which was built as a retreat for Queen Victoria and Prince Albert, in a very quiet part of the Island. We remember Black Gang Chine, where there was a model village. At Alum Bay we marvelled at the impressive cliffs and coloured sand. The Island has no doubt changed out of all recognition, but we enjoyed the peaceful atmosphere.

In the same year we had booked a camp site at Aberdaron, North Wales for the August Cadet Camp, the farm also had Bed and Breakfast

Water Patrol, Rhoscolyn

accommodation, so we decided to take Mother with us to stay at the farm.

The farm was on the hillside, overlooking the bay and just opposite was the camping field, it was a delightful site. The cadets and officers, apart from Pat, travelled by coach, Pat brought Mother and Ricky in the

Ricky, Muriel and Kate (pot on leg) enjoying ice cream

car, which was quite useful to have for carrying provisions up the steep hill to the field. We had brilliant sunshine the whole week, spending a lot of time on the beach. Ricky would stand at the edge of the sea barking until someone would carry him out to a nearby rock then he would swim back! One day we had a lovely surprise when the Vicar and Alison (our President) paid us a visit, they were very popular with the cadets.

Will they ever get the tent up?

Wales is popular for camping, in spite of the weather often being variable and in 1967 we went to Oxwich, near Swansea. This was quite a long journey by train but everyone enjoyed it. When we arrived at the site, to get to the field we had to walk through the muddiest farmyard we had ever seen! We soon found an alternative route! But whatever the weather, we could always bring out the best in the cadets and they never let us down.

In 1968 we went by coach to Rhoscolyn, on Anglesey, a lovely quiet site about half a mile from the sands. One of our junior cadets, eight year old Kate had an accident just before the camp, and although it was only a minor break, she had a pot on her leg. Her twin sisters were going to camp and it was her first camp, she was desperate to come, so we relented, fortunately she was quite small and Skip became an expert at "piggy backs"! We were again blessed with dry weather, but we had a shortage of fire wood! One day we had walked to the sands for a picnic, we didn't stay too long as there was a cold wind and we suggested on the way back, they should collect some fire wood. Imagine our horror when one section came trotting back to camp carrying a shiny wooden Yacht Mast! Take it back we cried before anyone sees you, they had no idea it was part of a yacht.

So it was a double quick trot back to the beach!

We liked to spend as much time as possible with Mother, who was now in her late 70's, and not in the best of health with Angina, Glaucoma and Osteoarthritis to name a few, but she was a good sport and enjoyed travelling and seeing different areas of Great Britain. In the late 60's we went to Norfolk staying at Mundesley, near the Broads, in a small hotel on the sea front. On the lawn, in front of the hotel, they had two tortoises tethered by chains to give them a good exercise area, they were fascinating.

Mother with her cousins in Wales

Pat had previously been to the Broads on a day trip, when she worked for the Local Authority, the Deputy Medical Officer used to arrange day trips for the staff, but it was the first time for Mother and Muriel. We all enjoyed the boat trips, including Ricky who was with us. Another time we went to the South Coast to West Wittering for a lazy, sunny holiday.

In 1969, two cousins, one was over from Canada, came to stay with us and we took them for a long weekend to the Bay Hotel in Rhosniger, whilst we were there we went to Caenarfon. It was just after the young Prince was invested as Prince of Wales in the Castle Grounds and we were able to see the decorations and memorabilia on sale, we purchased a rather nice Commemorative Plate, which we still have. It was a happy, enjoyable break for the cousins who did not have the opportunity to visit such places.

On the way home we drove through a thunderstorm and had to stop, Mother was sitting between the two cousins, who were scared of storms, they were wearing dark glasses with their coats over their heads, they looked so comical. They were a lively pair and when the storm had subsided, there was lots of laughter and they started singing for the rest of the journey home.

About this time Muriel decided to go to night school for woodwork and she made a magazine rack which is still in continuous use, followed by a bed table which is still among her souvenirs, but so far has not been used.

Finally she started making a bedside table out of Red Marante Wood, but the classes finished before she could complete it.

Mother with her cousins in Wales

The good news was that a few years later our neighbour Ernest was bored and jumped at the opportunity to finish it for her. Muriel has it in her bedroom, a useful piece of furniture!

For our 1969 camp we went by train to Rhosniger and it was perhaps a good job that we ordered a meal on the train, because we arrived in a deluge of rain! The campsite was about half a mile from the station and it was all 'hands on deck' to pitch all the tents. The rain continued on and off for three days, enticing the campers to have 'breakfast in bed'! But when the sun came out on the fourth morning, we were on the golden sands, for a sand castle competition. The Inspecting Officer came on the Wednesday at 1.00pm, and fortunately it was fine, giving us a chance to get everything 'ship shape'.

Waiting for the train

Although we would have liked to see a bit more of the sun, the cadets took it all in their stride and would be ready for the next camp!

For some time we had realised that changes were taking place locally and globally, the attitudes of people seemed different. There was an increase in bullying, children were growing up sooner. Some thought this was due to mothers going out to work leading to "latch key" children. We had very little support from our leaders who seemed devoid of new ideas. Our Mother had instilled in us 'that a thing worth doing is worth doing well'. We were fortunate with our Cadet Division and on our own volition we started a Junior Section. It was a benefit being able to have an annual camp, which was excellent in character building for those cadets who were responsible for a section of six in a Bell tent. The cadets had always been keen to enter competitions, but that lost its sparkle when there were only two or sometimes three entries. There seemed to be so many petty rules and regulations and we felt we could not continue much longer.

		TELEPHONES 37 and 50
		THE MEAT STORES
		ABERDARON

19 May 1970

M *St John Ambulance Brigade*

B OT. OF J. R. JONES

lbs.	ozs.	Nett Weight sent out	@	£	s.	d.
5		*Lamb Legs*	/6.	1	7	6

07055

		TELEPHONES 37 and 50
		THE MEAT STORES
		ABERDARON

30 May 1970

M *St John Ambulance Brigade*

B OT. OF J. R. JONES

lbs.	ozs.	Nett Weight sent out	@	£	s.	d.
5	.	*Brocure Steak*	7/-	1	15	0

07059

Camping in Aberdaron. Note the prices!

We decided to have a camp in May 1970, which could be our last cadet camp, we booked to return to Aberdaron, a favourite campsite. The Inspecting Officer, whom we had met previously was thrilled to visit us again, he was like a breath of fresh air and so easy to talk to. We had a most enjoyable, happy camp!

There seemed to be a degree of jealousy creeping in and the crunch came for us, when an Area Officer said the Brigade must always come first not the Church! We had always been taught through the Code of Chivalry, that service to God comes before anything!

We discussed the options with the parents and cadets and with their backing it was agreed we should all resign on July 31st 1970. We knew we must provide an alternative for the cadets, this was emphasized by the parents and the church who backed and supported us, so we agreed to form a new group called 'Knight's Templars'. The inaugural meeting on the 11th September 1970 was held in a party atmosphere with over 70 present, we sang Folk songs, looked at the last Camp slides and partook of an enormous Cow Pie and Pea supper, followed by apples and orange juice.

After supper, the Parents' Chairman announced that they had organised Insurance Cover under a Group Personal Accident and All Risk Insurance for 75 members.

We then talked about our plans for Junior and Senior Knight Templars and the older group Young Adventurers, our Motto was "For God and my Neighbour" the Meetings to be held on the same night and time.

We then had to start raising funds, but before we continue with that, there was another exciting event!

Pat received an invitation from the British Commonwealth War Memorial Fund, to attend a Silver Jubilee Afternoon Party at St. James's Palace on November 25th at 3.30pm, guests were asked to be seated by 3.20pm. The Queen Mother was Patron of the Fund.

> BRITISH COMMONWEALTH NURSES
> WAR MEMORIAL FUND
>
> Silver Jubilee Afternoon Party
> at St. James's Palace
> on November 25, 1970, at 3.30 p.m.
>
> _Mrs P. Calleo_
>
> Entrance from Marlborough Road

I was able to attend and it was a delightful afternoon in surroundings you don't have many opportunities to see.

The Queen Mother was in attendance and we all had our photograph taken with her. Whilst we were being put in our positions, there was a commotion at the entrance to the room as a corgi came running in, chased by a red faced butler, the corgi ran straight to the Queen Mother and sat beside her. The Queen Mother turned round and told us that he had come to tell her it was his dinner time!

Pat at St. James's Palace

The corgi sat by the Queen Mother to be included in the picture, the butler beat a hasty retreat!

Fund raising is always difficult and it is finding something different and saleable. By chance we found an advertisement about a kit for making Christmas Crackers, so we sent for a sample pack to find out what was required. We thought it was within our capabilities and it was something Mother could help with.

The boxes for the completed crackers came in flat packs of a hundred which you made up into boxes, with a staple at each corner. The fillers came in gross packets, crepe paper, ready cut, in different bright colours of our choice, strips of thin ready cut card to give the cracker support in the centre, jokes, paper hats, snaps (to go bang), a variety of different presents and pictures to be put on the front of each cracker. Included in the kit were metal cylindrical formers and a hank of special strong thin string. Muriel and Mother would assemble all the items ready for the next stage.

The string was attached to a board and Pat sat on the floor to hold the board firm, she held the other end of the string, rolled the prepared cracker round the formers, placed the string above the first former, pulling it tight to make one end of the cracker, removed the string, put the fillers in at the open end, applied the string above the second former to tighten the second end to make the cracker.

To complete it, we stuck a 'Christmasy' picture on the front, the crackers were placed in the box and secured with shirring elastic using a large hole sewing needle to pierce the box, finishing with a knot, put the lid on and 'Hey Presto' a professional box of crackers ready for sale! This might have sounded a bit complicated, but when we got into the swing of doing it, we soon had the first hundred ready. We continued making these, beginning in September each year, ready for Christmas right up to the early 1980's when we were raising money for the Northern General Special Care Baby Unit, more about that later!

To get back to the Knights Templar's we had a very busy time up to Christmas 1970! We held a Fair in November, the K.T.'s had been busy making items for sale and we made £40.00. The money was towards Christmas presents for the 30 old people in the district. We packed the parcels on the 11th December, taking them out on the 18th. As we had a lot of members we divided into two groups. We sang carols at each house and gave them a parcel and a bowl of bulbs. The K.T.'s had been practicing a nativity and on the 19th performed this at the Old People's party at St. Gabriel's Hall. On December 21st the parents provided cars to first take us to Brincliffe Towers old people's home, the ladies were waiting for us in the dining room, where we performed our Nativity and sang carols, giving presents of bath cubes, then we were driven the five miles to see the gentlemen at Parkhead House again performing our Nativity and giving presents of home made truffles and mints.

21

On Tuesday 22nd Pat took Five K.T.'s and Y.A.'s by car to nine visits including Lodge Moor Hospital and Woodbank Old People's Home, which were far flung.

Then on Wednesday 23rd and Thursday 24th we visited two more large Care Homes for the Elderly and on each night performed our Nativity, sang carols, giving out presents and talking to the residents who thoroughly enjoyed the chit-chat.

Our numbers for the two K.T. sections and the Young Adventurers for those in their teens were maintained. They were always interested in camping activities, and cooking both indoors and outdoors. The K.T.'s were pleased when their new flag was blessed, making them able to join in with the other flag bearers at church parades. The flag which had been beautifully handmade by Skip (Pat),was admired. The summer months were particularly busy starting in May! The Vicar had asked six people from the congregation, including Pat, to each give a sermon for the six weeks after Easter, on their 'Experience of the Resurrection' culminating on the sixth week with a Flower Festival. The K.T.'s were excited that I was giving a talk on the final evening of the Festival, which they had been able to help with, and, of course, Mother was thrilled to be there.

I found that preparing my 'Experiences in the Gift of New Life' quite an onerous task, which required a lot of thought!

Needless to say I was nervous when I mounted the pulpit steps and looked at the large congregation, with all eyes on me as I gave the opening prayer:- 'Lord, speak to me that I may speak the precious things thou dost impart, and wing my words, that they may seek, the hidden depths of many a heart. Amen.'

Then I was into my talk, which I had carefully prepared and all went extremely well.

I was also asked to take the prayers after I had given my talk. I started with a special prayer dedicated and used by Midwives' for over two Centuries. I received a very appreciative letter from the Vicar.

ECCLESALL PARISH CHURCH

Reverend JOHN N. COLLIE, M.A.
Tel. 0742 360084

ECCLESALL VICARAGE,
RINGINGLOW ROAD,
SHEFFIELD
S11 7PQ

Miss P. Callis,
29, Gisborne Road,
Sheffield. 11.

18th May, 1971.

Dear Pat,

It is with very profound gratitude that I
write to thank you for your address on Sunday evening -
an address to which Dr. Jackson makes specific
reference in a write-up for Spur which he has done
on the course of Easter sermons. I am so thankful
to you for agreeing to speak on that occasion and I
am sure that none will forget the impact of what
you said.

With renewed thanks not only from me but
from the Church as a whole, and every good wish,

Yours very sincerely,

John Collie

Thank you letter to Pat

23

K.T.'s at Wetton Camp

Pat had contacts with the Ambulance station, frequently giving talks to the Ambulance men on 'Emergency Midwifery' a popular subject! They reciprocated by giving First Aid talks to the Senior K.T.'s and the Y.A.'s which resulted in 3 Y.A.'s being successful in the Bronze section of First Aid for the Duke of Edinburgh's Award.

From 1971 to 1975 so much happened that we will attempt to put it in chronological order beginning with the first K.T.

Whitsuntide camp. We decided that we would camp nearer home, choosing Wetton in Derbyshire, this was so that one of us could get home easily, if required. We had a full day's outing on the Wednesday visiting the Tramway Museum at Crich.

On the Thursday night we had a big Camp Fire, when several parents, villagers and our friends from the Ambulance Station who also brought our Mother with them. They all brought a mug as requested for their cocoa! It was a very entertaining evening thoroughly enjoyed by all. Everyone said that a country camp with different types of activities was just as good as a sea side one.

It was also the year when decimal coinage was introduced, 15th February 1971, which was very difficult to get used to. By chance we have found the Butcher's invoice showing that he was only completing the first and third column, to use his invoice book up.

We had one other canvas Camp in June 1972, which was at Wardlow, even nearer home. The coach broke down going up the hill to Eyam with steam billowing out, a nearby house let us have water to fill the tank, so we were soon on our way. Unbelievably it was one of the wettest and windiest camps, but we all survived and we even had a visit from one of the Curates who came to help.

Pat was the next calamity in our story, in July 1971 I was busy preparing a sitting room at the hospital for a meeting and pushing a settee out of way had a low abdominal pain and a lump appeared! I had to take a class of students, leaving them with some questions to answer.

To cut a long story short, after seeing a female Gynaecologist, I was dispatched home to let the family know what had happened, collect belongings and Muriel had to take me back to the hospital to go to theatre at 2.00pm. It was thought it could be an ovarian problem, but instead it was a bleeding fibroid, so I ended up with a hysterectomy!

The class I had left with some work to complete, thought I had gone on a half day and when they found out what had happened they came to see me with a present.

In those days, a post-operative stay in hospital was much longer, and it was the ninth day before I was allowed home.

I was off work for almost seven weeks, during that time we went to our favourite holiday hotel at Rhosniger for a week in lovely weather.

Our much loved poodle Ricky who was 13years old died on the 4th April 1972. Mother was heartbroken and we had to spend as much time as possible with her, the house was so lonely without an animal. One day when Mother was out in the car with Pat, they stopped at an Art Gallery, looking at

Koblenz

numerous pictures. Mother really liked a woodland scene, so we placed an order. The picture had pride of place in the lounge and was much enjoyed, when we moved house it still has pride of place in our lounge, it's a loved picture that never dates.

We decided to take advantage, not having an animal, to take a holiday abroad, so we booked a cruise in September on the River Moselle, starting from Koblenz in West Germany. We were given instructions for parking the car at Folkestone from where we had to take the cross channel ferry to Calais. The ferry was busy and noisy so we went to the Purser's office to see if a cabin was available and there was, which enabled us all to have a rest. On arrival at Calais, we boarded the coach, meeting our fellow passengers, for the journey to Koblenz.

Koblenz

The journey was rather long, fortunately we were good travellers and the coach was comfortable, we had a stop enroute, but it was 10.30pm and pitch black before arrived at Koblenz and boarded our Cruise Boat. After we had been welcomed onboard we were shown to our cabins, Pat sharing a cabin with Mother, in case she wanted something during the night.

We learnt that the boat had been one of Hitler's Boats, which had been converted to a cruise ship, although it wasn't a large boat, it was quite comfortable. We cannot remember the number of passengers, but it could only have been about 30 or so, as there was only one sitting for meals. We stayed the first night moored in Koblenz, so we were able to see our surroundings.

After breakfast we left the moorings and started our journey down the River Moselle. The weather was variable, but there were bright periods. The area was famous for the vineyards, which were prolific on the hillsides. We stopped at two vineyards during the week where we had the opportunity to taste the wines and make any purchases.

It was probably on the second morning, I had left Mother putting her elastic stockings on, whilst I had gone for a wash, when I returned, Mother was in fits of laughter, a gentleman had come into our cabin, only to disappear quite quickly!! At breakfast, the gentleman who had made the 'faux pas' was full of apologies for mistaking the cabin! He and his wife were a friendly couple, who we corresponded and met up with after the holiday. Another day we stopped at a larger village and we saw a rather nice coffee shop, with delicious cakes, so we ordered three coffees and cakes, they were very delicious but when the bill came, Mother could not get over the fact that they were the most expensive cakes she had ever had!

On the River Moselle

The week soon came to an end and we were back in Koblenz.

It was in the late afternoon and Mother was happy to stay on the boat with another friend, so we walked up the hill to the Castle giving us good views. Muriel was persuaded for a quick descent to go on the ski lift, she was quite convinced that she would lose a sandal, but she landed safely. We then went to look at the shops, suddenly we were aware a man was following and whistling us, so we went into the nearest shop! It so happened to be a shop with items in carved wood.

We had a good look round and we both liked one of a man playing a 'squeeze box', so we bought it. By that time the path was clear and we hastened back to the boat.

The meals on the boat had been very good and varied. It was a good job we weren't vegetarians then, as the last meal we had, and had never had before, was veal! We packed our cases ready for an early start in the morning

Peter Mynah Bird

after breakfast. The coach took us to the ferry and before long we could see the white cliffs of Dover in the distance and we were saying goodbye to our friends.

We collected the car and started our journey to stay overnight with Mother's cousin in the village of Houghton, Huntingdon. The village is delightful with many old cottages, the Great Ouse River passes near by, as well as the 17th century Houghton Mill which was taken over by the National Trust. The river was made navigable with locks and the area is popular with artists and during the summer is busy with pleasure boats. Our cousin Colin's wife had recently died and we were pleased to be able to spend a couple of nights with him before returning home.

We realised we could not have another dog, but we did wonder about a bird! Just before Christmas in a shop on Abbeydale Road we saw a Mynah bird chattering away and it seemed an ideal Christmas present for Mother, so we purchased Peter Mynah Bird! He was a year old and very good at saying 'Hello Peter' and an excellent 'wolf whistler'.

When we let him out of his large cage to have a good fly round, he was very tame, sitting on our hands and on the window ledge looking out at the birds in the garden. Mother was really thrilled with him. He was also very curious and liked investigating and picking things up.

Mother liked the occasional cigarette, we impressed on her not to let him out when she had a cigarette. The Curate visited Mother one day to find Peter had got a cigarette and he had quite a job catching him to recover it!

Pat had enjoyed four years in the teaching department, but when a post became vacant for a Nursing Officer in charge of the Labour Suite and the Antenatal Clinic, I saw it as a chance to be more involved in the practical side of midwifery and my application was successful. I was particularly interested in 'Preparation for Childbirth' and although I had to give up taking classes for the National Childbirth Trust, it opened interesting avenues. There was a lot of unrest in the 1970's caused by the introduction of the 'Salmon Report' which changed the traditional nursing career structure, by altering the titles from Matron down. The Government made cuts in the floor workers, but put more money into employed Managers. In 1973 there were strikes, due to the cuts that had been made, affecting the ancillary staff. A major problem was the laundry, the nursing staff and other volunteers with the help of a local firm donating a twin tub washing machine, set up an effective laundry service for the three weeks strike. Some washing was sent to laundries outside the city. Mothers were discharged early, others brought their own sheets and baby clothes The staff were brilliant through this difficult period.

Both of us were members of our Professional Organisations, Pat's was the Royal College of Midwives, which I joined on becoming a practicing Midwife. Regular meetings were held, where we frequently had a speaker, which helped to keep us up to date.

The RCM was a much older organisation than the Dental Surgery Assistants Professional Organisation, only dating from the 1940's, when they were the 'Cinderellas' of the Dental profession and had to fight for recognition. In the first 25 years very significant progress had been made, including moving to their Office at Poulton Le Fylde and employing a full time General Secretary, Miss Jean Smith who was a mine of information and represented us on various committees. After I had been Treasurer of our local branch for several years, in 1968 I became the National Treasurer, which I enjoyed very much. In 1973 it was the North East Branch's turn which covered Sheffield, Newcastle Upon Tyne and Leeds, to provide a nominee to be President for the coming year. I was nominated for the honour and was delighted to accept. This would be a very busy year for me, so one of the members from Scotland volunteered to stand in for me as Treasurer for the year. The installation at the AGM was to take place at Roehampton, London, during the Easter break. Mother was so excited and we arranged that Pat would bring her down on the Saturday for the Annual Dinner, staying overnight for the installation on the Sunday Morning, returning home after lunch. Pat had the task of buying Mother a long dress for the occasion! We were fortunate that there was a very nice dress shop, locally at Bannercross and they had a lovely long dress that fitted Mother perfectly, also a suitable one for Pat! We had a great time and Mother was so proud.

l stayed an extra night and I was able to go for a trip on the River Thames organised by the local branch, and it also enabled me to meet and get to know more members which was important.

I wrote a President's Travelogue for our magazine, which was published quarterly. Fortunately most, although not all, of the meetings, were at the weekends and for those in the week, I had a tolerant boss who allowed me the time off.

My first visit was to Glasgow, travelling in my small Fiat 'Flaming' June for me, was almost a reality, when on Sunday the 3rd, I literally burst over the Scottish border in a cloud of smoke! Fortunately by my side was an AA. telephone box. An hour and a half later, an oil bespattered AA patrolman and myself diagnosed a 'jumping dip stick', which responded to a degree of firm handling and I was on my way after telephoning my hostess that I would be late. Apart from bringing up the rear in a Youth Parade, near Glasgow, I arrived safely at the member's flat at 9.30pm where two other members were waiting

Mother at Roehampton for Muriel's installation as President

to welcome me! It was quite a relief to get up on a sunny Monday morning, with no thoughts of work and better still to be 'chauffeur' driven on a tour of Glasgow and its environs, including the airport and the new Erskin Bridge, followed in the afternoon by a visit to a busy dental practice. The members of the Glasgow section met at the Headquarters of the BMA (British Medical Association). The Business meeting and my talk concluded, we were joined by members of the Local Dental Committee following their meeting in another room, for the social part of the evening and the traditional Scottish refreshments. Unfortunately the time passes all too quickly. On my way home in perfect weather and delightful countryside, I could reflect on the enjoyment of meeting so many old and new friends.

The following weekend I was on the road again to Birmingham to be met at the boundary and escorted to a member's home, only to be found once more covered in oil!

Fortunately the man of the house improvised with a rubber bung and yards of sellotape and Eureka! Mobile!

Muriel's first speech as President

The weekend started off with a Dinner on the Saturday evening with the opportunity to meet and chat with most of the members. This was followed by a large gathering at the Central Clinic, when 20 Certificates were presented to successful Candidates from the 1972 examinations who had been unable to get to the conference. A member of the Panel of Examiners presented them. I was amazed at the distance some of those receiving a certificate had travelled, including Derby and Gloucester. Is there potential in these areas for new sections to being formed? I was pleased to be able to speak on this topical subject.

Pat, Mother and Muriel

My journey from Birmingham took me on the M6 to Southport, where, along with our Association Secretary, we had been invited to the B.D.A Annual Conference which was a great honour. This was just the beginning of my year as President and I had many more visits to make.

Meanwhile all the Sheffield members continued to prepare for the 1974 Annual meeting. This included having some money raising events, to cover the extra cost of hosting the four day event. We held a Barbeque and Car Treasure Hunt organised from our home at the end of July, which was very successful. A letter was sent to the Lord Mayor requesting a Civic Reception, in the Town Hall on Friday the 12th April to welcome the Conference. Then a letter to the Master and Mistress Cutler inviting them as special guests to the Dinner on the Saturday. Both requests were accepted.

Accommodation had been reserved, for those members and friends who wished to attend. It was customary to present a small gift to all those attending, so Stainless Steel Letter Openers were purchased. A Conference hand book was produced for the four days giving an Educational and Social programme

The Conference started in good style on the Friday, with the coaches arriving to take us to the Town Hall for the Cocktail Reception. We were welcomed by the Lord Mayor and Lady Mayoress. Following the welcoming speech, and Muriel's response to the City of Sheffield for their Hospitality, the Lord Mayor and Council Members gave the members a guided tour of the Town Hall.

Muriel proposing a toast at the dinner

The Annual Dinner, on the Saturday, in the company of the Master and Mistress Cutler, the President of the British Dental Association and Muriel had invited her boss, who was to make one of the speeches. After a lovely meal, it was time for the Toasts, Muriel first gave a toast to Her Majesty the Queen, followed by proposing a toast to The Company of Cutlers in Hallamshire in the County of York, a unique Company, not known to many of our members and visitors.

Muriel's boss giving a 'witty' response

Muriel continued by giving a "potted history" of The Company of Cutlers which was formed four centuries ago, compared to the Association of Dental Surgery Assistants, less than 40 years old. They like us, started with a Voluntary register in 1614 and it wasn't until 1624 before statutory registration commenced.

The Association of Dental Surgery Assistants are hoping to achieve this in the not too distant future. After further historical details, the toast to the Company was made, the Master Cutler then responded.

Further toasts were made to 'Our guests' and the final toast was proposed by Mr Armitage, (Muriel's boss), The President and the Association, to which Muriel responded. The Mistress Cutler was then invited to present the Certificates and Awards to the successful Dental Assistants. The official part over, the dancing commenced with Mr Armitage taking Muriel on to the dance floor.

On the Sunday, following the Members' only Annual Meeting, at 11.15am all were reconvened for the Installation Ceremony of the new President, from the Midlands branch. I gave my Valedictory Address, in which I quoted a saying used when I had been installed as President.

Think big and your deeds will grow,
Think small and you will fall behind,
Think that you can and you will.

I am delighted that these words have become a reality for two members, who have each formed a new section for our Association, one in Derby and the other in Gloucester.

During my year I was privileged to visit all the branches in England, Scotland and Wales covering some 2,500 miles. My one disappointment was that due to the situation in Northern Ireland, a visit was not advisable, but we are delighted that representatives have come over from Northern Ireland

Easter Bonnets

for the Conference and we ask them to convey to their members our heartfelt sympathy in their trials and we send our hopes and prayers for a speedy, peaceful settlement to their problems and restoration of law and order.

I then installed our new President for 1974/75. The lunch at 1.00pm was in Honour of our new President. Following lunch, the coach arrived to take members to the Police Headquarters to watch the training of Police Dogs, this was a popular visit and very interesting.

Muriel installing Eileen as the new president

In the evening the hostesses, showed two short films, one of Sheffield and one of the Yorkshire Dales. This enabled those in the Easter Bonnet Parade to get ready for the judging by the journalist from 'The Star' newspaper, there was lots of fun and laughter with the parade. The 32nd Birthday Cake was then cut and pieces distributed to everyone.

The team of hostesses at the Sheffield AGM

On Easter Monday at 9.30am we boarded the coach to take members to see the beauty of the Derbyshire countryside, journeying via Moscar Moor, Lady Bower Dam to Edale, then on to Castleton. Here some members visited Peak Cavern whilst others toured the numerous shops selling Blue John and other stones. During the morning, in typical Derbyshire fashion, there was open air village dancing. Leaving Castleton we journeyed through Hope and Hathersage to Grindleford where we dined superbly at "The Maynard Arms" on the traditional Roast Beef and Yorkshire Pudding, rather ironical as we were just in Derbyshire. Our coach brought us back to Tapton Hall over Ringinglow with splendid views of the City of Sheffield.

To round off the weekend those remaining visited the Crucible Theatre on Monday evening to see a performance of R.B. Sheridan's 'The School for Scandal'. This was acted on a modern "Thrust Stage" which allows 1,000 people in the audience to have a perfect view, and it was enjoyed by all.

It had been an amazing and enjoyable four days which ran like clockwork, mainly due to the team of hostesses, who wore a green sash throughout the weekend, which easily distinguished them. So our thanks go to those in the photograph for a job well done.

Following the last Canvas Camp in 1972, we realized that Mother's general health was deteriorating and we couldn't both be away overnight, which a Canvas Camp required.

We had seen an advertisement for youth groups to go on Canal Holidays, so we went down to Long Eaton to see the owners of 'Three Fellows' carrying/camping boats and were very impressed with what we saw. The 70 foot Long Boats, which had been working boats, consisted of a Motor Boat and a Butty Boat, pulled by the Motor Boat, but had to be steered.

The boats were owned by Herbert Wood, who had been born on the 'cut' (canal) and he had converted them into Camping Boats. The Motor Boat had facilities for the owner, but the rest of the boat and the Butty Boat was fitted with bunks, cooking facilities, washing and Elson toilet, there were places on the canal where you could empty the toilet, or you may have to resort to digging a hole!

Life jackets were provided. It all seemed perfect for us and we booked the Motor and Butty Boat for the Whit week holiday.

The Butty Boat for our first canal holiday would have his partner Neil to negotiate the steering. It was agreed that Pat would be on the Boat for the first half of the week with Muriel taking over for the second half of the week, our friend Margaret would accompany us.

The K.T.'s were very excited to be going on a canal, which was a new experience for all of them.

Our first week was in 1973, the numbers were less, so the parents were able to take the K.T.'s by car and we took Mother with us in our car to Long Eaton where we would embark, Pat went on to the boat for her first half of the week and we arranged to meet up for the change over on the Welford Arm. Those who had come to see us on our way, gave us a good send off!

Life on a canal was entirely different from Canvas Camping, although the K.T.'s all had to take it in turns with the cooking, washing up, keeping the boats tidy and many other jobs. They also had to learn about the Locks and

Double lock

Steering the Butty Boat under the watchful eye of Herbert and Neil. We had ordered food in advance, which was waiting for us on the boat, to give us a good start, but then we had to rely on the village shops. Of course, the parents had provided a cake for their child to bring!

Canal boats travel much slower, (approx. four miles an hour), but there is always plenty to see of the views, wildlife and wild flowers. On a quiet part of the cut you may be fortunate to see the shy Kingfisher, with its beautiful colours, dart out to catch a fish, or you may see a water vole.

If there were two locks in fairly close proximity you could get off the boat and walk on the tow path to the next lock. There were houses by some of the locks, which had originally been for the Lock Keepers, but only a few now housed Lock Keepers who were very helpful, friendly folk.

On this part of the 'Cut' the locks were mainly double ones, which meant that the Motor Boat entered the Lock, then the Butty Boat was pulled in by the side of it, on leaving the lock the Motor Boat had to make sure the Butty Boat

Flight of locks

was firmly attached. There were also single locks with only room for one boat at a time, the Motor Boat entered the lock, the Butty Boat was held by the crew, waiting for their turn. The lock would either have to be filled or emptied and then the Butty Boat was pulled into the lock to be eventually united with the motor boat. On approaching a lock you had to be prepared to fill the lock if it was empty by opening the paddles to let the water in, when the lock was full you opened the gates to allow the boat in. Sometimes you had to wait in a queue until the lock was free.

As Youth Leaders, we enjoyed the opportunity of talking to the children and it was amazing the interesting conversations we had, and the youngsters enjoyed learning more about us and our work. In the evening we could sing camp songs, or have card games, Beetles, Quizzes, and I Spy, were all popular. We had encouraged them to take a book to read during quiet periods.

We would always pass the time of day with towpath walkers and passing boats.

Our timetable for the day was to get up at 7.00am followed by prayers on the towpath if it was fine, at 7.30am, then breakfast, lunch was between 12noon and 1.00pm, tea was when we found a suitable place to moor for the night.

Neil at a single lock

Depending on the weather we could go for a walk after tea, if there was an open area we could have a ball game or 'hide and seek' before cocoa, washes and bed, finishing with 'taps', a sung good night prayer.

The following year we went to Stone in Staffordshire, when Muriel was on the Boat for the first part of the week. Margaret had a prior engagement, so it was arranged that Pat would take her on the Monday to join the boat at Fradley. It had rained at the weekend and Muriel was in process of getting dried out! Pat was due to change places on the Wednesday and our elderly neighbour jumped at the chance to have a ride to Stone which he thoroughly enjoyed. As it was an early start, Mother stayed at home with the neighbours keeping an eye on her.

For this holiday Neil was in charge of Motor Boat and the older KT's steered the Butty Boat, which they enjoyed, it was very quiet on the Butty Boat with no engine, just gliding along.

Stone was a more commercial area and I remember the canal being quite close to the road. On the route back we stopped at Rugely on the Wednesday night, then went to Burton, where Herbert Wood met us and joined us for some soup, he then left and we continued making our way back to Sawley on the Friday in lovely sunshine, although the wind was strong on the River Soar. For the last night of our holiday we were moored and had a campfire on the riverside. On Saturday Muriel and the parents arrived to take us all home.

We also made a tentative booking for a K.T.'s holiday at the end of August 1975.

Meanwhile, we must go back to 1973/74 to our family holidays.

It struck us that a canal holiday might be a good idea for Mother and we would be able to take Peter the Mynah bird with us. So we made enquiries at a Skipton Boat Yard, and there was a small four berth boat available in September, which would take us on the Leeds and Liverpool Canal. So we booked the boat, Mother was quite excited by it.

It was quite an easy drive to Skipton, where we boarded the boat, Mother and Peter seemed quite happy with their accommodation! There were a few boats going out at the same time and the owners accompanied us for a little way, to ensure we were happy with the boat.

An advantage of a canal holiday was that Mother had us with her all the time, and there were always new views of interest. The first night we moored quite early and the following day we had to negotiate our first lock. That was when we nearly got into trouble, which taught

Peter happy with his accommodation onboard

Muriel and Mother on the canal

us our first lesson. Don't let the bystanders help, take your time to make sure everything is correct! Soon we were on our way! Lesson number two, the wind can play funny tricks with a small boat, turning the boat completely round, facing the opposite way! With a little more wind and a bit of manoeuvring, we soon learnt the tricks of the trade! On the second day we moored by a lovely, peaceful and grassy flat area and after having a meal had a short walk before settling down. We stopped and visited some of the villages enroute and were able to buy provisions. During the week we got to know a couple who had started off at the same time, but their boat was a petrol driven cruiser, which was a very lively boat continually requiring more petrol! He was always looking for a petrol station! Of course at that time boating was a relatively new past time. But we had a good time with lots of laughter, arriving safely back at the boat yard at the end of the week.

In the early part of 1974 we were kept busy with Muriel's President commitments, but in the summer managed to have a long weekend in Scarborough, staying at the Royal Hotel. It was situated on the cliff top, almost overlooking the sea. Mother thought it was marvellous because it had all the niceties of an old-fashioned hotel. Of course that was in a different era of hotels, looking at it 40 plus years on, you would be forgiven if you didn't recognise it. We had a lovely weekend, benefitting from the sea air.

During this period, Mother's glaucoma wasn't controlled, we visited Miss Jones, the Ophthamologist, privately in her home at Ranmoor. Despite all the drops, her pressures remained too high. Mother was admitted to the eye ward, but unfortunately she had a heart attack whilst there and couldn't have the operation. When I went to see Mother, one of the doctors was beside her bed with some medical students and she asked me about Mother's routine first thing in the morning? I said that she had a cup of tea, with a small tot of Whisky before she got up. The Doctor turned to the students saying, you see, these patients know what is good for them, whisky would be a vasodilator to get her going! She came home and after she improved Miss Jones decided it would perhaps be better if she was treated as an outpatient. So a day was arranged when Pat could take her and all went well with the operation. I asked Miss Jones when she would be able to go home and she thought it might be simpler if I took her straight home. It didn't take long to get home, although Mother was a bit shivery, she soon improved in front of a warm fire and a hot drink. The operation did help together with the drops.

We were very fortunate having two cars and we always worked, when possible, on opposite shifts, so either of us could take her out for a run and encourage short walks, which she enjoyed. She loved the countryside and occasionally we took her further afield and had a meal out.

Our Doctor was excellent, visiting Mother every month, always coming around 1.00pm when he knew one of us would be in, we also left a note if we needed tablets, in case we had been delayed.

Muriel had always wanted a Greenhouse, so around this time we had a rectangular one erected on the top lawn and started growing tomatoes. This was also another interest for Mother. Muriel was interested in organic gardening and she joined the Henry Double Day Association known as HDRA.

In the midst of all this, we had our weekly meetings with the K.T.'s which we enjoyed, although it became more difficult finding activities which they didn't do at school, even down to changing a plug! It was a bit frustrating to be told 'we do that at school'!

They revelled in cooking, which seemed to be one of the few things missing from the School Curriculum! Outdoor cooking was top of the list, also indoor cooking making fudge, toffee and similar goodies.

We also encouraged them to make small teddy bears from a simple pattern, these were sent to children abroad.

As we had done for many years we went round singing carols and giving a present to the elderly, the housebound and those living on their own at Christmas time.

For Christmas in 1974, Pat's colleagues made sure that she had Christmas day off, as it could be our last Christmas with Mother. We always tried to keep everything as normal as possible, going to Church on Christmas Eve for the Crib Service and carols. We had the meal prepared in advance with the turkey ready for the oven before we went to the Christmas Morning service. Then we set the table for dinner, with a bottle of wine, the best glasses, cutlery and plates for this special day. After dinner we waited for the Queen's speech at 3.00pm then, we watched TV and had '40 winks'!

Between Christmas and the New Year, there were often Dances in the Church Hall, one year when we had visitors for the evening to stay with Mother, we went to a fancy dress dance. You had to dress up representing a song, Pat remembers being dressed as "Night and Day" half in a day dress and half in nightclothes, half my hair in curlers and half styled. It was great fun, unfortunately we don't seem to have a photograph! Muriel cannot remember her outfit!

Mother always liked to see the New Year in. It had become traditional for many years, having a few friends in for a meal, then, from about 11.00pm we would join in with the celebrations on the television. In those days it was great to watch, with lots of fun, singing and laughter.

Just before midnight, the pair of us would go out by the back door and when we heard the chimes for the New Year we knocked on the front door, when Mother opened the door we chanted:-

"A Happy New Year, a Happy New Year,
A pocket full of money and a cellar full of beer,
A horse and a gig, and a good fat pig,
To last you all next year.
A hole in mi stocking, a hole in mi shoe,
please could you spare me a copper or two,
if you haven't a penny a ha'penny will do
if you haven't a ha'penny God bless you."

Mother would then cross our hands with silver and we would put a piece of coal on the fire. Then glasses were filled to propose a toast to the New Year and hot mince pies were given. Before our visitors departed for home, we would sing "Auld Lang Syne".

One Year we were waiting for the chimes, when, coming up the road was a tall, young gentleman, beautifully dressed as a fairy, with a wand, who wished us a happy New Year. (We still let the New Year in, but now it is first thing in the morning rather than staying up!)

Our family was small, with cousins in America and Mother had a half brother in Blackpool, he had two children, Barbara who was a similar age to Muriel and Peter, who was a few years younger. Peter married and had two children, a boy and a girl, who will be mentioned later in the book. We were in touch with Uncle Alan and Peter by telephone and at birthdays, and they were aware that Mother was not well.

We carried on, doing as much as we could to give Mother a happy time and when walking became a bit too much, we got a wheelchair, but she was never very happy being pushed !

If she had been in the wheelchair a few minutes, she would say I think I'll walk a bit and we would be pushing the empty chair! One of the last outings was to Edale, on a quite road, which she enjoyed. The summer of 1975 was very hot.

Last picture of Mother at Edale 1975

One of our regular visitors was Florence, who used to look after us both in the 1930's. She had married and initially lived in the Derby area, but following the death of her husband, came to live in Todwick, to be near her sisters. When she heard that Mother was deteriorating she came and stayed with us. The heat in the house was unbearable and we had a fan going all the time. Our Doctor visited on 1st August, to say he was going on holiday, but he had asked his partner to call and see Mother on the Saturday, so that he provided cover, for when the inevitable occurred. On the Saturday and Sunday she sat in the wheelchair by the open bedroom window, such was the heat. During the night she seemed a little restless and Pat carried her to the toilet, then laid her in bed, she had a spoonful of medicine and some ice cream and went to sleep. The end came peacefully at 4.30pm on the 4th of August just eight days before her 84th birthday. The doctor came to certify the death and one of our clergy came to say a prayer, followed by the undertaker. Later on we took Florence home, it had been so comforting having her with us. We both had the following day off to sort out the arrangements, but we were back at work the next day, as Mother would have expected. The funeral service was at Ecclesall Church followed by Cremation. Our uncle and cousin had come from Blackpool and Florence, so the five of us went home to have the meal we had prepared. Our uncle and cousin then drove home.

Before taking Florrie home we had a short walk in the cool of the early evening, which was lovely.

Mother's ashes were buried, as we had promised, near to Canon Jordan's grave, in Ecclesall Church Yard.

Part IV

Decisions to be Made

We had to reorganise ourselves, there were still the K.T.'s to consider, although the numbers had fallen, for which we could only blame ourselves. Mother had been our priority.

A canal holiday had been booked for the last week in August and we would both be able to go, this was fortunate as Margaret was unable to come due to her father being very ill. We rang Herbert to ask if Peter the Mynah bird could accompany us and he said it would be fine.

The weather remained perfect and we really benefitted from the break. The K.T.'s were so good, it was a pleasure getting to know them even better, everyone had a great time.

We both had a holiday for two weeks in October partly due to having worked overtime and a canal holiday was booked. The week before we were due to go, Pat had a bad cold and we had been to church in the morning, so after lunch we decided to go for a long walk. By the time we had reached an area known as Park Head, we decided to go back through Ecclesall Woods. On entering the woods we met a friend with her dog on a lead plus another dog. We said we didn't realise she had two dogs, she said she only had the one dog and the other one had followed her, she hoped it would follow us! We said that much as we would like a dog, we were both working long hours. We carried on with our walk and when we reached the main road, there was the dog! Well we couldn't let it get run over, so Pat made a lead from the belt off her coat and the dog trotted beside her. When we arrived home we rang the Police Station, but nobody had reported a missing dog! It was quite happy to settle down in our house and have something to eat! The next morning Pat

Fun on the canal

walked the dog, then took her to work in the car. The Midwifery staff were all dog lovers, but none felt able to take on another dog! On the way home I called at the Dogs' Home, (leaving the dog in the car), to ask if anyone had reported a missing dog, and no one had. One guess, yes, we would keep her, she was a lovely mongrel, her new name was Heidi, and we went to a dog shop to get all the requirements for her and suitable for two weeks canal holiday!

Peter the Mynah bird and Heidi quite liked each other, sharing the back seat of the car was no trouble, even though the cage took up quite a space. A canal holiday is a quiet, relaxing break, you go through delightful countryside at four miles an hour. Heidi only had one slip up, when she jumped off the boat without a lead, but she only wanted to perform a 'call of nature' and we soon got her back. She loved being on the deck and if we were on a straight stretch nothing was better than sitting on Pat's knee when she was at the tiller. She soon realized she had landed on her feet, finding us! The holiday benefitted us both, to be ready for the winter.

Heidi helping Pat with the steering

Our next door neighbours had known us from birth and looked on us as 'relatives'! On making an extra covered area for the second car, we had extended it making a door between the two houses, giving an easy, dry access, to both houses, which was useful as they were all in their '80's'. On returning from our holiday, we took them all for an afternoon run to Dove Dale. At that time we only had a normal size car, to fit in five adults and a dog, so we couldn't go far, but they were so thrilled with the outing, it was a pleasure taking them.

Peter and Heidi were good friends!

Gradually the K.T. numbers continued to dwindle, we did the Christmas visits with carols and

Our three neighbours with Muriel and Heidi in Derbyshire

presents. In 1976 we continued with our meetings as usual, but with smaller numbers. Then we had a telephone call from Herbert Wood asking if we could help out by providing a few of our K.T.'s to man the 'Butty' for a week with a new group, with no canal experience. We were delighted to help out and I took four of them down and stayed with them for a couple of nights to ensure they were alright with the cooking, sleeping accommodation and steering. I remember cooking a large meat and potato pie for Skipper Neil and the five of us! I then returned the following Saturday to transport them home, after an enjoyable week. The K.T. numbers had dropped so much we decided not to continue after the summer break. We had the cupboards to clear out in the Hall and a meeting to discuss what to do with the money in the bank. We decided to leave it where it was until we found a worthy cause for the donation.

In 1976 we decided to exchange one of the cars for a Fiat Motor Caravan, which we felt would be more useful now we had a dog and a Mynah bird! Then one Saturday in March, we had to send for our GP urgently to see Muriel due to a bladder problem, this had happened previously and she had ignored it, but now it was worse. Our excellent GP managed to sort it out and found there was a lump causing the problem, entailing a visit to our lady Gynaecologist and on March17th Muriel was admitted for a hysterectomy, which revealed that a large fibroid had been pressing on her bladder. During the operation she had quite a heavy blood loss, so was given a blood transfusion, which unfortunately, she had a reaction to and her face was the colour of a 'turkey cock' so it was discontinued, but regardless of that made a very good recovery.

Shortly after this, at Easter, Muriel had the Annual meeting of the Dental Nurses Association to attend in Liverpool, in her role as National Treasurer. The Sunday morning Annual General Meeting was the important one. As Muriel was unable to drive being only three weeks post op., Pat took her in the new motor caravan on the Sunday morning in time for the 10.00am meeting, leaving after lunch.

Our motor caravan on it's first outing into Shropshire

We were keen to try out the motor caravan, so we went on to Trentham, where we understood there was a camping area. It was a very quiet site, so we stayed there for two nights. Due to Muriel having to take it easy, one of the campers helped Pat put up the awning, which was attached to the motor caravan and we enjoyed our first introduction to this different style of camping. On our next free weekend we went to Beeston, Cheshire, camping on a small campsite with only two other ladies in a caravan. They introduced us to the Camping Club of Great Britain, telling us about all the advantages of being Club members. Nearby, there was a Craft exhibition, showing how to make candles and the equipment required to make them. This opened a new hobby for Muriel, which she passed on to the K.T's before the group ceased to meet. It was a lovely area, but it was sad to see so many rabbits with Myxomatosis.

On returning home we joined the Camping Club and have, so far, been members for 41 years.

We wanted to help out with a friend of Mother's, they had both been in the N.A.A.F.I. Canteens in the First World War and had remained good friends, we called her 'Auntie' Emily, she lived in Ripon and owned a Fishing and Gunsmith's Shop. She had two daughters, Brenda worked in banking and the elder of the two, Joyce, was a qualified teacher, who then felt the call to join the Anglican Order of Nuns in Bristol. Auntie Emily had never reconciled that Joyce had done this and she had lost a daughter! Recently, Joyce, (Sister Bridget), had been put in charge of the Retreat House at Glastonbury, a beautiful, large house, in spacious grounds. To cut a long story short, Auntie Emily felt she wanted to see Joyce in her working environment, but was nervous about it. Sister Bridget wrote to her mother, inviting her to stay for a fortnight. So it was arranged that Auntie Emily would come by train to Sheffield and we would meet her, then we would go down to Somerset. It was dark when we arrived and parked the motor caravan in a grassy area and we all went into the house for a meal, washed down with Somerset Cider! When we got back to the van, to get ready for bed, we heard a rustling and chattering noise and looking out of the window, saw a family of hedgehogs, as though they were welcoming us or perhaps they were saying 'we live here'! We returned home the following day, having arranged to come back in a fortnight to take her home. When we arrived back, the hedgehogs once more greeted us. The nun's had been so kind, Auntie Emily had thoroughly enjoyed her stay.

We took canal holidays in March or October, leaving the summer months for camping. One March we took Gary, our cousin's son on the canal. One day it had been raining and we moored by Drayton Manor Park, Muriel in wellingtons was mopping the floor and slipped into the canal. We pulled her out, very wet! Before going below deck, she had to strip off her wet clothes, to Gary's delight! He made sure everyone knew about it. Later, we took his sister, Marila, plus Grandfather, (our uncle) on a larger boat, to Chester and had an accident free week! More canal experiences later.

With the motor caravan we had more space to take our neighbours for treats, the first one was a day trip to Stoke Bruene, which was by the canal and there was an interesting museum. It was a gorgeous sunny day and we had taken a picnic lunch, finishing with ice creams. It was lovely to see them so relaxed and happy.

On another occasion, their nephew David, who was a Vicar in the south of England, wrote to tell us he had arranged to do an exchange holiday with the Dean of Ripon Cathedral.

He wrote to ask if we could spend a day, with him and his mother, Hilda who lived with him. (Mabel, Annie and Hilda were sisters.) We had known David and his brother, who were of a similar age to us, from childhood, when they visited their grandparents next door.

We were again blessed with a lovely summer's day, when all five of us and Heidi had an early start to reach the Dean's House in time for lunch. We enjoyed a pleasant afternoon, in the large garden, prior to our journey home. We also had an invitation to take Mabel to Whitby for a weekend, where her friend Paddy Toes had retired to. She had lived with Mabel next door, during their teaching days, so we knew her very well. Her flat was on the first floor, with a good view of the sea. There were plenty of walks for Heidi and Paddy knew the area very well. On the Saturday, we had a delightful tour in the car of the whole area. Paddy's brother and family, lived nearby and invited us for Sunday lunch before returning home.

Our neighbours all died within five years of each other, they were all characters in their own individual way.

Ernest was married to Annie, he and his two brothers had a building firm and there are many houses in Sheffield bearing the name Malthouse. They lived in a lovely 'show house' overlooking a park. He was a golfer and very good at drawing quick sketches, he did one of Muriel. Latterly when the business failed, they came to live with Mabel. He became ill and was admitted to hospital, the inevitable came when we had a phone call at 4.00am to urgently take Annie to the hospital, but he had died when we arrived.

Mabel was a very well read lady, we understood she was the first female to gain a place at Sheffield University.

She became a teacher and taught for many years at Greystones Primary School, she never married and lived with her parents, becoming their carer as they aged.

Mabel at Stoke Bruerne

One night, when she was well into her 80's, she felt ill and was worried she hadn't changed her will. The only paper she had upstairs was some thin card, which was used for part of the packing when buying silk stockings, and she wrote out her new will on the thin card, ensuring that, on the following morning, she had two people to witness her signature, it was all very correct.

Mabel died very suddenly and we were away, arriving back to find that the funeral had been arranged by Annie and a neighbour, with a Methodist Preacher, although she was Church of England and her nephew David would have liked to take the service but was not asked! We were both executors for her will and her Solicitor took us to a Commissioner for Oaths to swear on the bible that this 'unusual will' was her last Will and Testament and that we could vouch for the two witnesses. The will was proved.

It must have been about three or four years after Mabel died, that Annie died. In the meantime, she had a 90th birthday party at a restaurant in Dore. She also had a friend called Phyllis, who came to stay with her and we all enjoyed a New Year's Eve party at our house, with several neighbours.

Annie's financial state was just her pension. Her friend stayed with her for most of the time, but Annie was getting more confused and bedfast, Phyllis was unable to care for her. Whilst Muriel stayed with Annie, to await the doctor, Pat took her friend home, which is yet another story!

Phyllis lived at Walkley and when I opened the door to put her luggage in, the house looked as though she had been burgled! I went back to the car and spoke to Phyllis, who was somewhat embarrassed and it transpired that this was how she lived! Eventually we managed to get a social worker to help her.

Meanwhile Annie kept changing between hospitals, care homes and nursing homes, with each change we had to go back and forth to the Social Services, regarding payment for her care in the nursing homes and although it was time consuming, they were helpful. On November 5th 1983, Bonfire night, she was transferred to the Royal Hallamshire Hospital, from the nursing home. We went to visit in the early evening, Heidi was scared of fireworks, so we took her with us in the car and parked in the hospital underground car park, hoping it would be quiet. Annie was laid on a reclining chair in the sitting room and the staff asked us to wait until they put her to bed, this done, we went to her room, just in time to see her die. We called the staff who couldn't believe it! But it was true! On returning to the car Heidi was fast asleep.

We mentioned earlier in our story about the changes which were occurring in all walks of society, which did not seem to fit in with our Christian upbringing. Muriel had always tried to ensure that young children were given basic knowledge, enabling them to differentiate what is good and what is bad. The Sunday School teachers always tried to move with the times, although they felt they were being pushed in different directions and the changes envisaged didn't seem right. Some of the teachers, including Muriel and her deputy Wendy felt the time had come to move on to "pastures new". Our friends, the Hanson's suggested we should move around until we found a church where we felt comfortable. Wendy went to St. Augustine's Church at Hunters Bar and we went to St. Andrews Church, Sharrow, where we were welcomed and made new friends.

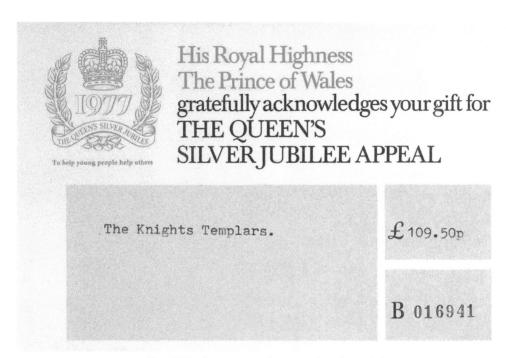

His Royal Highness
The Prince of Wales
gratefully acknowledges your gift for
**THE QUEEN'S
SILVER JUBILEE APPEAL**

1977

THE QUEEN'S SILVER JUBILEE

To help young people help others

The Knights Templars.   £109.50p

B 016941

The K.T.'s donation to the Queen's Silver Jubilee

A short note from the late 1970's.

In 1977, the Queen's Silver Jubilee Appeal was announced, which was particularly involving young people, and it seemed like a worthy appeal for us to donate the K.T.'s money that was still in the bank. Following a meeting with the K.T.'s parents, it was agreed to send the £109.50p to the fund, and the account was closed.

In June 1977, we decided to go to Scotland for two weeks in the motor caravan, including Heidi and Peter the Mynah bird, now the important members of the family! We journeyed on the north east side of the country, stopping overnight at one of the club sites, then making for the Cairngorms, where to Heidi's delight, there was snow on the hills for her to roll in, at the beginning of June with the sun shining! We stayed three nights. We continued up the north east seeing beautiful scenery, our next main stopping place was Tongue. On our first day we went to John O'Groats, and on arriving back at Tongue, we realised the motor caravan had developed a clutch problem and the garage had to send for a spare part, so we had to stay an extra two nights, but the weather was fine, so we enjoyed the walks and being lazy. Once we were mobile, we went along the north coast, passing the Queen Mother's retreat home, the Castle of May. Our next delight was coming across Scourie, a small, quiet place, with one hotel. We camped on the grassy bank, just above the golden sands, the sea was crystal clear, it was bliss! Due to being delayed in Tongue, we had to press on south via the west side staying at Moffat, continuing through Gretna Green, Penrith, Appleby and back home. It had been a lovely journey but we didn't have enough time to explore, so Scotland was high on our list for return visits.

Our holiday in the Cairngorms, Scotland

Fancy snow and sun in June

Muriel's Dental Association had their Head Office in Poulton-le-Fylde, their meetings were at weekends and on a few occasions we were able to go in the motor caravan. We had relatives in Blackpool, so whilst Muriel was at the meetings, Heidi and I would visit the cousins, often taking Marila, and sometimes accompanied by Uncle Alan, long walks into the Forest of

Bowland or the Lake District. We had an awning, which was very good, but not as steady when we took the van out. On one occasion we arrived back to find the strong wind had played havoc tearing the awning.

On a previous campsite, we had been interested in a Dandy trailer tent. The motor caravan was a bit small, quite heavy on petrol and following the awning problem, we decided to go to the manufacturers, near Wigan and see if it would be suitable. It seemed ideal for us, so we ordered one.

We then had to do a part exchange of the Fiat Motor Caravan, for a Fiat Panda car which would be suitable for towing the Dandy.

The back seat would fold down giving us more space for Peter's cage and Heidi, also it was a two door car, which made it extra safe for the pets and we had a tow bar fitted.

The exciting day came to collect the Dandy and we were given instructions about the tow bar and arrived home in fine style, until we realized it was a problem to get up the slope and into the garage! We had a good neighbour across the road, who tried to back it up, but it was too steep.

Eventually, it was all hands on deck and we pushed it into the garage, this happened a couple of times, then on the advice of Bob, he fitted a "block and tackle" with yards of rope, which solved the problem.

Both of us were kept busy at work, putting in long hours, we seemed to live on salad type meals, which we prepared a week in advance.

Muriel will now tell you how she was enjoying the challenges of a busy dental practice. My boss wanted to open a Private Practice at his Broomhill Residence, which was next to the Royal Hallamshire Hospital. This allowed another full time dentist to be employed at the Holmhirst Road practice, with a trained dental nurse, also a trainee, to learn office procedure. For myself, I was still able to do one evening a week, with a Specialist in Orthodontics and fortnightly, on a Saturday, two General Anaesthetic sessions, one being in Sheffield, starting at 8.30am, followed by the 2nd session at the Bolsover practice, finishing about 12.30pm. I looked forward to these hands on sessions.

Normally, I would be found in the far end of the office, engrossed in book keeping, preparing for the weekly visit to the bank. This involved paying in to the practice account, money received from the patients and working out how much I needed to withdraw for the wages. In the late 1970's staff were paid weekly. There were also dental reps to see and orders to send.

You never knew what would happen next, it could be a blocked spittoon or a hand piece requiring repair. But it was all in a day's work!

Quite often, patients would require an explanation of a procedure and the cost. We also did a lot of dental education, teaching a child how to brush their teeth, and talking to the parents about fluoride applications, or even looking after a baby or young child, whilst the mother was having treatment. One had to be 'Jack of all trades' to keep everyone happy!

One evening, in the late 70's, one of the associate dentists in the practice at Woodseats, visited me at home with her husband, she made a surprise statement, saying that she was negotiating to purchase the Holmhirst Road practice from the boss. Before the final decision was made, she wished to check my position as the Practice Manager and if I would be prepared to stay. I replied 'yes' we do know each other and would be able to work as a team. Her husband David was interested in the move and would support his wife. I would expect changes with a new boss, but said I could cope with that. The first plan was to re-site the dental laboratory into a temporary accommodation. The spare bedroom at her in-laws home was offered and was ideal. The extension room would be built on the small piece of land which adjoined the office. It would have been impossible to do this until the laboratory had a new home for about six months, the technician, Gerry, was happy with this arrangement.

As soon as this happened, the vacated room would be cleaned and decorated and this room would become a surgery for the new boss. We went to view the equipment at a showroom in the Midlands. The order was placed and the delivery date given when the installation would be done. It was all very exciting and work progressed steadily with Mr Sanderson senior, overseeing it.

It was in the middle of a busy afternoon, that a patient came to tell me he had knocked my little Fiat 127 into a tree, the car was a write off! Fortunately no one was injured. Mr Sanderson senior ferried me around for a few days until I had found a replacement car.

Things soon got back into order, Gerry the technician was back amongst us in his new laboratory, next door to the office and we now had four surgeries working full time.

The attic was the staff room and we tried to make a ten minute coffee break, every morning. Admittedly, it didn't always work out!

Pat now mentions the training courses attended by those of Middle Management Grade. Myself and the Middle Manager from the theatres, were sent on a course at Newstead Hospital, in Nottinghamshire, this was for two weeks, Monday to Friday and because of the distance it was residential. From what I can remember, the course was organised by hospital administrators. We were probably fortunate to go to this one as the later ones were more complicated and high powered! I remember having to produce 'Action Projects' on a subject pertaining to our work, before the end of the course, and I wrote a lengthy practical project, which seemed to have impressed them. I still have the report I received, which said that my report and work, was more like that of a colleague than a course member student! On another occasion, managers spent a weekend at Losehill Hall Centre, Derbyshire, which was quite enjoyable, but so much of what we were doing, was common sense, it seemed such a waste of time and money!

On a lighter note, in 1981, we were celebrating the Hundredth Anniversary of the Royal College of Midwives. Prior to the event, we had been asked if we could think of ways to celebrate the occasion. The Sheffield Branch with the help of a Silversmith designed a Presentation Teaspoon, I still have two of the spoons, the bowl of the spoon, was enamel with the College insignia and the dates. I seem to remember that we sold several hundred spoons. There was also a plate designed through the College, for £30 as a limited edition, we have one hanging in our dining room and still have the box it came in.

There was a Hymn written for the occasion "Vita Donam Dei" 'Life is the gift of God'. A rose tree was specially grown, a pretty salmon pink colour, a competition was held to choose the name, "Breath of Life" was selected. We planted a tree in our garden and it was

Reception at St. James's Palace attended by the Queen

lovely. When we moved from Sheffield to Castleton in 1986, we took the tree with us and it blossoms prolifically, we have the garden open to the public once during the year, visitors are always interested to hear about the "Breath of Life Rose".

We had invitations to an evening reception in London, at St. James's Palace attended by the Queen, who was shown the Centenary Plate and signed a book, she then walked amongst us all, it was a lovely event.

The Sheffield Branch also had a Centenary Reception at the Town Hall, Sheffield, by the invitation of the Lady Mayor and her daughter, who was her Consort. Nearly all the branch members were there, including our very new male President. I was Chairman of the Branch, so I gave a speech thanking the Mayor and City of Sheffield for the Reception and I presented three Rose Trees to be planted in the Sheffield Botanical Gardens. It was a relaxed, friendly evening, thoroughly enjoyed by all.

In the Maternity Unit, there were plans for updating the Special Care

Pat No. 16 on the Star Walk

Baby Unit, for which we would have to raise an appreciable amount of money, also, there was a need for an Obstetric Theatre, next to the Labour Suite. Currently, if an emergency caesarean section was required, we had to run with the patient on the bed, down the long corridor to the General Theatre!

We were fortunate to have a retired Consultant Dr. Rhind, who took over the task of raising funds for the Special Care Baby Unit, and the staff were all encouraged to help, obviously this had to be done in our own time.

I decided that I would enter for the "Star Walk". This was an annual event, the women's section had to undertake a speed walk of 9 miles, over quite a hard route.

I got a lot of sponsorship so it was important to do well. Prior to the day there was a training session anyone could attend, which I found helpful.

I practiced as much as I had time for and I got a reputation for speed walking down the corridors!

The big day arrived, Whit Holiday, Tuesday June 1st 1982, Muriel took me in the car to Leppings Lane, where over 300 were waiting for the start of the race, my number was 16. It was a fine warm day and I got off to a good start up the notoriously steep hill and I knew I had to keep up the pace all the way.

Muriel and Heidi went to cheer me on along the route, at places where she could park. The atmosphere was amazing with everyone cheering us on. Eventually after going uphill and down dale we entered Hillsborough Park, with the end in sight.

Out of the 303 walkers, I was placed 13th, with a time of 1 hour 51 minutes 47 seconds! I had a further excitement, there was a Sealed Handicap for walkers over 35 years of age, when this was worked out, I was 1st in the Sealed Handicap reducing my time to 1-37-17. On June 7th I received a letter from the Star confirming that I was a prize winner and inviting me to the Gala Evening with the other prize winners, on June 18th.

My prize was three graded Casserole dishes, all three are still in

From Northern General to The Moor!
The Incubator Push

The football teams

frequent use, but much more important, it had raised £500 in sponsorship for the Special Care Baby Unit Appeal.

There were two more fun events, an Incubator Push and a football match. The Incubator push was on a fine Saturday morning, using an obsolete incubator. One of the technical staff, the lightest one, made it so that he could just fit in with his head showing, with a dummy in his mouth. All the men were dressed as nurses, the females as babies, wearing nappies. Around 40 assembled outside the Maternity Unit, there was lots of fun when we started pushing the incubator from the hospital to the Wicker, through the town centre and down to the Moor, about three miles, collecting money on the way. It was a very successful money raiser.

Pat, Dr Rhind, Radio Sheffield and Sr. Mudge

The football match was on the Sunday, the male football team were hampered by wearing nappies, even pinning them to their shorts didn't really help. The female team was made up of midwives, nursing auxiliaries and anyone who proffered their services. To be truthful, there were some fouls, but everyone had a great time. Who won? Shall we say it was a dead heat!

There was one other event that I was involved with, in an obscure way, I towed one of the smaller Walls ice cream vans from the centre of Sheffield, to sell ice creams at the Dog Show, which attracted large numbers. One of our staff, Barbara, who went to Crufts each year, offered to organise the show, with her friend Pat Chapman, whose flat coated Retriever was Supreme Champion in 1980, she agreed to be judge, bringing her famous dog for all to see. There were lots of entries and at the end of the afternoon, our organiser and judge were exhausted, but happy that it had been so successful. Towards Christmas, there was a good sale of our boxes of Christmas crackers, they all sold very quickly for the appeal.

The appeal was aided by Radio Sheffield making 1981 their 'Appeal of the Year'. They were frequent visitors to the unit.

The money rolled in, often we were asked to go to a pub or club, usually this was after work about 9.30pm, but it was good to be able to thank the groups for their efforts. It was a busy time in the unit, together with the usual routine.

I also received a request to present a paper at the Midwives AGM in July 1983, the theme was A Statement on Antenatal Care, my subject was 'Midwives' Clinics'. Previously one of the Obstetricians and myself had lectured a group in Staffordshire on a similar subject, this time it was in the University of Essex.

We decided to combine it with a holiday at West Runton, and we would go to Essex for the day. This worked out very well. There was one excitement that occurred on the campsite, the day before we were due to come home, we were having breakfast in the awning and I saw something moving under the groundsheet, Heidi was with us, so we held her collar.

Gingerly we rolled back the groundsheet and there were two Harvest mice nests with young babies! Of course everyone wanted to have a look at them. We made a square cardboard bed round them with plenty of grass and they seemed quite happy. Since then we have never used a groundsheet in the awning, which is a good thing really, because they do make a mess of the grass.

The appeal had reached £220,000, sufficient to convert part of a ward next to the Labour Suite, for the new Special Care Baby Unit. This was completed, together with the Obstetric Theatre, in 1984, when HRH Princess Anne came for the Opening Ceremony.

To go back to four days before Christmas in 1983, the social worker came to the Labour Suite with a problem arising from a woman who had to be admitted. There were four children and a 14 week old puppy, fastened to the table leg!

They could provide care for the children, but they couldn't find anyone to have the puppy, all the kennels were fully booked, due to it being close to

Toby

Christmas! After much pleading, that it was only for two weeks, I succumbed and telephoned Muriel to make sure she didn't mind. On the way home I called at the vets to check that the dog was healthy, only to be told it had signs of rickets! Heidi accepted him and 'Spot' settled in very well, eating all the good food the staff kept bringing for him. The owner never asked after the dog, in the end, I suggested that as the dog was on an expensive diet, would she let us look after him. After some thought, she said 'you can have him'. What a relief! We immediately renamed him 'Toby' and he lived with us for 13 years.

We were very happy worshiping at St Andrews Church, the Vicar, Wilfred Hudson and his wife Barbara, were such a happy, hard working pair. After we had been going for about three weeks we were invited to be on the list for reading the lesson and joining the Sidesmens' rota, a few weeks later we were asked if we would like to help with flower arranging. This was something that we didn't know much about, but we had our friend Val, who owned a florist shop in Dore, she also had classes in flower arranging, which we joined.

Our good friend, Alison Hanson, gave us two beautiful books on flower arranging with strict instructions 'to read and digest'! We worked hard at it and by May 1984, we had our first Flower Festival 'The Living Church' there were 16 arrangements beginning with 'Living Water' in the Porch, we had lots of help, including children.

Wilfred invited the Bishop of Sheffield to come and he brought a visiting Bishop from Africa who was staying with him they were so easy to talk to, as you will see from the picture.

Muriel, Bishop of Sheffield, Bishop Rev. Hudson from Africa and Pat

Other arrangements included Baptism, The Family, Babyhood, Childhood, Teenage, coming of age, Marriage, Silver Wedding and Old Age as well as biblical scenes. It was a great success!

On November 14th, Muriel had a very important letter waiting for her on the doormat when I arrived home for lunch. It was from 10, Downing Street, to say:-

'The Prime Minister has asked me to inform you, in strict confidence, that she has it in mind, on the occasion of the forthcoming list of New Year Honours, to submit your name to The Queen, with a recommendation that Her Majesty may be graciously pleased to approve that you be appointed a Member of the Order of the British Empire'.

I had to fill in a form to say I was agreeable and I would receive no further communication before the list is published. The letter was to be treated in the strictest confidence, telling only your nearest relative. It was only later that we found out it was due to my service to the Association of Dental Nurses.

Our New Year's Eve party was a very happy event, when we could let our friends know the good news!

On January 10th, a letter came to say the Investiture would be on Tuesday 12th February, giving all the details. Our Uncle was asked if he would like to come with us, and he was thrilled. Then we had to decide on what both of us would wear, including a suitable hat, for this grand occasion, bearing in mind it was February and 1985 was an extremely cold year. We made arrangements at the travel agents to book accommodation in a London Hotel for the 11th of February.

The dogs were booked in kennels for two nights and we arranged for Peter the Mynah bird to be looked after by a neighbour.

A day to remember.

We were up early for breakfast and then it was back to our rooms, to get ready for the taxi, which would take us to the Palace. The taxi driver was surprised when we told him to go through the main gates so we could get out at the entrance to the courtyard. It was sunny but very cold, and to get to the Main entrance we had to walk through a sprinkling of snow and ice.

We were directed to the cloakroom and then I was shown to the recipients room, meanwhile, Pat and Uncle went to their seats in the ballroom where the investitures are held.

The recipients are organised into groups, according to the award they are to receive. There were about ten to 12 in each group and when it is your group's turn to be called, the Gentlemen at Arms accompany the group through the rear doors of the ballroom to an ante room, where you wait to be presented. There is a dais at one end of the ballroom, with two thrones, beneath a velvet canopy and the Royal Insignia, the remaining three walls had upholstered couches in tiers. The band of the Grenadier Guards, in the Minstrels' Gallery played a delightful selection of music throughout.

Five Yeomen of the Guard took their places on the dais which heralded the entrance of the Queen, accompanied by two Gurkhas and various court officials. The National Anthem was played and the Investiture Ceremony commenced. Altogether about 150 people received their awards – the ladies being in the minority. The Home Secretary read out the names of the recipients, at following investitures the Lord Chamberlain would do this.

The Queen speaks to all the recipients in a very personal manner, asking about their work and offering her congratulations. At the conclusion the National Anthem is played, the Queen leaves the ballroom, followed by the Gurkhas, Yeomen of the Guard and court officials. Then we all dispersed, to meet up with relatives and friends in the cloakrooms, passing the Guards standing like statues, to have the official photographs taken in the courtyard.

We walked to the Palace Gates, under the scrutiny of the tourists, to hail a taxi to take us back to the hotel.

The fairytale morning was over, but the memories will last for ever.

Muriel in her uniform - a picture requested in a letter from Downing Street

CENTRAL CHANCERY OF THE ORDERS OF KNIGHTHOOD
ST JAMES'S PALACE, SW1A 1BG
TELEPHONE - 01 - 834 2837 & 2838

INVESTITURE A   10th January 1985

MADAM,
I am commanded to inform you that an Investiture will be held at Buckingham Palace on Tuesday, 12th February, 1985, at which your attendance is requested.

I am desired to say that you should arrive at the Palace between the hours of 10 o'clock and 10.30 a.m. and this letter should be shown on entering the gates of the Palace and at the Grand Hall Entrance of the Palace, as no other card of admission is issued to recipients. Cars may be parked in the inner Quadrangle of the Palace under police direction. A Car Parking Label is enclosed herewith.

If desired, two guests are permitted to accompany you to watch the Ceremony, and tickets for them may be obtained by making application on the form enclosed herewith which should be returned to me as soon as possible.

The only exception to this rule is that, if a recipient wishes to bring with her her husband and two sons, or two daughters, or a son and daughter, a third ticket will be issued, but in NO circumstances will a fourth ticket be issued.

DRESS
(a) Serving Officers and Other Ranks of the Women's Royal Naval Service, Women's Royal Army Corps, Women's Royal Air Force and Members of the Police Force and Fire Brigades should wear the dress laid down in the regulations of their respective Service. Orders, Decorations and Medals should not be worn.

(b) Civilians may, if they so desire, wear the uniform of the Civil Organization or Service to which they belong; otherwise they should wear Day Dress. Orders, Decorations and Medals should not be worn.

I am, Madam,

Your obedient servant,

D. H. C. Rice.

Major General

Muriel was awarded the MBE for her work with the Association of Dental Nurses. I was their National Treasurer for many years, also representing them in London on the Joint Committee of Dental Surgeons and Dental Nurses, working to gain Professional Registration as Dental Nurses. I was eventually elected as the first Dental Nurses Chairman of the Committee for a three year term of office. All this work was entirely voluntary

Part V

Searching, Finding and Retiring

After all the previous excitement, we now decided that the time had come to leave Gisborne Road and look for pastures new! The road was getting busier and we could do with an easier driveway, so we started scanning the papers for suitable housing in Derbyshire. When we both had a weekend off, we would take the Dandy trailer tent plus two dogs and Peter the Mynah bird to camp at the Youlgreave Camping Club site and scour the estate agents to find something we liked! We got quite good at assessing houses and bungalows, there always seemed to be something wrong, but 'Rome wasn't built in a day' and we persevered. Well over a year later, we found a cottage in Bakewell, which had been completely renovated and we loved it, but if we had really thought about it, we would have realized it was completely wrong for us. Fortunately, our solicitor made us see sense, so the search continued!

A week later, on a Saturday, it was my weekend for the early shift, mid morning Muriel telephoned to say there was a dormer bungalow for sale in Castleton, she would go and have a look, if it was a possibility, we could go out when I got home. In the middle of the afternoon, I had a telephone call from a near neighbour to say that Muriel's car had broken down between Ringinglow and Hathersage and she was waiting for the AA.

I was able to leave work and went to find her, still waiting for the AA, she had seen a breakdown vehicle on the top road, obviously looking for her, but she was on the lower road, eventually with much arm waving they arrived and her car had to be towed to the garage, so necessities were transferred to my car and we proceeded to go to Castleton, somewhat later than she had arranged with the owners, but they were very nice about it, when they heard what had happened and showed us round. We couldn't believe it, it was everything we wanted, a garden, a double garage, two bedrooms, the entrance was flat, the toilet and bathroom were downstairs, which didn't bother us – it was made for us! We asked if we could bring a friend to see it and expressed an interest in the property. We took our builder friend on the Monday and he was pleased with the condition and negotiations commenced.

Our house was put on the market and we had three people interested, the agents offered it to one of the three, who accepted. Meanwhile, life in Gisborne Road was busy as there was no 'chain' on either side. The owners of 'Millcroft' were as anxious to move out as we were as anxious to move in! Muriel had been busy for some time, putting cuttings of cherished plants into pots. Our only sadness was leaving St. Andrew's Church where we had worshiped for ten happy years. Pat had been Deputy Church Warden for over a year and had found it interesting. We could hardly believe that everything had moved so quickly. The two tea chests that we had used when camping were brought down from the loft, cleaned and filled with items that we didn't think we would need; these were carefully wrapped in newspaper to protect from damage. We had a removal date booked in November, but a week before that, the policeman and his wife who were having our house 'backed out'.

So all was cancelled and our house was back on the market! We reduced the asking price on the advice of the estate agent. Then the right person came along and the sale was completed in six weeks, so we had one last Christmas and New Year in Gisborne Road and we were able to have a few friends in on New Year's Eve, amid the packing cases. We were eternally grateful to the previous owners of our new house for their patience and Ron even called at Gisborne Road to see if he could help by taking the trailer tent ahead and locking it in the garage for us. We had already been to the local skips to dispose of the rubbish, so we were fairly organised. The moving day in January was fine, but cold and the removal van arrived on time. They were a

The front of 'Millcroft'

cheerful pair of men, who got on with the job. They had a good laugh, that they had never moved a garden before!

Muriel took the two dogs in her car, calling at the solicitors in Hathersage, for the keys to the house, then on to Castleton to await the first van load.

The move went very well and after the last van load, Pat looked round to make sure we hadn't left anything and it was clean and tidy for the newcomers. Then, with Peter the Mynah bird in the car and various other oddments, we arrived at our new home. The neighbours came and welcomed us and George Bramall brought us one of his own homemade Bird Boxes to put in the garden

The previous owner was very sorry that he'd had an accident with the glass door leading to the utility, a local builder came and we asked him to replace it with a wood door rather than glass. The door wasn't a standard size so he had to make one to fit, which had to be glued to the original frame

Muriel and Pat
Choir girls!

and it was a week or so before it could be fitted. But 32 years on and the door's as good as the day it was made.

The next day it was back to work, we had to be up early for dog walking and extra travelling, but never regretted the move, when we reached the 'Surprise' with the amazing panoramic view of the Hope Valley, it was like going on holiday. Within a couple of days we had a 'Welcome letter' giving useful details about the village, this was done by Mr Braham, who was Headmaster at the village school and his wife Gill, who taught at the school, whom we soon got to know very well. We started going to St. Edmund's Church and very soon we were asked if we would join the choir (they must have been desperate!). It was one of the few churches where the choir wore purple robes and hats – so we were the 'purple perils'. Our neighbour, George, asked if we could ring Tower Bells, we said 'no' but we would like to learn! So we started going to the weekly practice night which we enjoyed, although we found it more complicated than it looks, particularly as the ropes were from floor level to the height of the church. Pat managed to break three 'stays' that is a piece of wood which stops the bell from going right over and was relegated to a heavy bell. Some weeks we went to Hope to practice on their bells, which were easier to ring and they had a ringing chamber, so the bell ropes were not down to floor level.

Garland Girls

Little did we know that we had moved to Castleton in a special year, as well as the Annual Garland Day Celebrations, it was the 900 years Anniversary of Peveril Castle.

Susan as Consort lived on our road

For the benefit of those who do not know about the Garland Festival, this special day is May 29th, unless it falls on a Sunday. Prior to the day, some of the village men fasten branches of sycamore, oak and elm around the four pinnacles of the church tower. The villagers go out the previous evening and early the following morning, collecting flowers to make the garland, lilac, bluebells, wallflowers and any other flowers from woodland, hedgerows and gardens. These are tied in bunches on to the beehive shaped frame, until the garland is a mass of flowers over three feet tall and approximately weighing half a hundredweight. A special posy is made and placed at the top of the garland, called "the queen", villagers wear sprays of oak.

The Garland King and Consort wear Stuart outfits, the Consort is now a young girl, who rides side saddle. Between 5.30pm and 6.00pm, they ride around the village bounds, then go to the host pub, where the Garland is hoisted onto the King's shoulders and the Castleton Silver Band strikes up the processional tune, the young girls, in their flower-bedecked white dresses, dancing the steps of the unique Morris dance and waving wands of ribbon. The procession stops outside each of the six pubs and puts on a display, whilst the landlord sends out ale for the band and lemonade for the dancers. After about two hours, the procession arrives at the marketplace and maypole. The King is led to the church gates, where the "Queen" the special posy, is lifted off the top of the garland. The King then proceeds to the church, where a bell rope is lowered and fastened to the garland, then hauled up and placed on the central pinnacle, where it stays for about a week. The children then perform intricate maypole dances.

The ceremony then moves further into the marketplace, where the King dismounts and places the posy on the War Memorial. The band plays and we all sing 'Abide with Me'. The band lines up and marches down Back Street, followed by everyone dancing to the procession music.

We were lucky in our first year, as Susan who lived on our lane, was Consort and we were able to see all the preparations.

The Peveril Castle 900th Anniversary Committee had organised eight days of events, from Sunday 13th July to Sunday 20th July 1986. The weekdays were particularly for and organised by the locals with a Medieval Market each day, the weekends were for everyone. We were all encouraged to join in, but it transpired that they were short of a Town Crier, Pat undertook this when she wasn't working. A very smart costume was hired as you can see from the pictures and it was great fun. Pat was also a Castleton Plod (quickly changing outfits and again when I wasn't working), this was for a murmurs play. Muriel dressed herself in Norman Style, participating in an evening of special readings in church and joined in with the parades. All the shops and houses were decorated and the villagers looked fantastic dressed in Norman, homemade costumes. As Town Crier, I had to direct visitors to the many items that were taking place, especially throughout the three weekend days.

Pat as Town Crier

The non-stop entertainment included The Castleton Play by the School Children, the Salamander Street Theatre, our own Castleton Plods, Morris Dancing, the Anniversary Parades, the W.I. with the Spinning Jenny, Fire Eating, Stilt Walking, Strolling Minstrels, Castleton Silver Band, Fortune Teller, Wirksworth Early Music group, Medieval Battles staged by Escafeld Medieval Society, Noah's Flood staged by locals, Musical Quadrille on Horseback, Pony Vaulting,

Castleton Plods. Pat on the left

Pat at our front door. The dogs wondered who it was!

Farming display, Falconry, Maypole Dancing, Rope Making, Lead Mining, the Stocks and Gymnastic Displays by Hope Valley College. On the Saturday night there was a Firework Display from Peveril Castle.

On the final Sunday at 9.15pm there was a Medieval Evensong, attended by many people all dressed in Norman Costume, followed at 10.00pm by a torchlight procession up to Peveril Castle. The torches were Tallow Flares and for those who are not familiar with the path up to the Castle, it is very steep and winds back and forth, so the effect was amazing. As we were standing in groups around the Castle, it looked ablaze in the clear night sky. Before we came back down, there was a short speech, followed by singing 'Happy Birthday' and 'Auld Lang Syne', we wended our way down, while the torches were still alight to guide us.

What an amazing start to village life, it was such fun and we joined in as much as we could and we were soon getting to know the locals and they got to know us.

We were able to invite friends from our previous Parish St. Andrew's, to come for afternoon tea, about 20 came, including the Vicar, Wilf Hudson and wife Barbara. They became lifelong friends, they loved the Hope Valley and visited us frequently.

In June and the first few days of July, we spent about 12 days camping near Criccieth and were blessed with good weather. The Lleyn Peninsular is very pretty and near the campsite there was a woodland walk with a river, which the dogs enjoyed swimming in. Getting the Dandy trailer tent in and out of the flat garage and drive was sheer bliss, and in October we went to Sussex to a wooded campsite at Graffhan, near Petworth. The two dogs were very alert as there were deer roaming.

Back at home, our efforts at campanology were beginning to improve, we rang for the first time before a service on Remembrance Sunday, continuing to improve by ringing every Sunday (when Pat wasn't working). Our new found talent was required for weddings in the area, as were our singing efforts and

The dogs swimming in the river at Criccieth

we got paid for doing it! Our earnings were going to a good cause, we had found a full set of hand bells, so we wanted to form a hand bell ringing team, but they had to go to the Foundry for quite a lot of restoration work which was quite expensive.

Our Garden.

Muriel was itching to be able to see what was in the garden, but it was early January, with a covering of snow. However we had two basic, urgent tasks to do. One was to make the garden secure for our two active dogs, the second, was to have a greenhouse for all the plants, to have shelter for the next three months.

The garden beginning to take shape. The bush in the middle of the lawn used to swirl around and we gave it away. When it was dug out, it was still in its pot

There was a long privet hedge across the front garden facing west. We took this out and on the neighbours advice we asked Alan a local gardener to put up a larch pole fence to extend from the stone wall in the corner to the double metal gates.

We then sought the advice of a Garden Centre, over at Moscar who knew the area well, for the most suitable greenhouse.

They suggested a hexagonal shaped one, to be fitted at the back of the house, it would look good from the kitchen window and withstand the winds. How right they were! We put our order in and the work was very soon completed.

We had two stone walls, beginning at the north east boundary, which passed behind the greenhouse, to the corner where it turned south and linked up to the larch fence. Both walls were in good condition.

There was already a concrete footpath all around the bungalow, with a low stone wall, this needed to be much taller to hold back the earth in a high border - this was Pat's job.

In the spring the area behind the garage was covered in bluebells. Prior to the bungalow being erected, the land was a 'croft', with an orchard beyond our stone wall. Muriel aimed to make an 'Organic' garden like we had in Sheffield.

The first year we spent clearing the ground, requiring a skip! We both collected suitable stones ready for building up the walls. More privet bushes were removed, the only trees left were a white lilac and two Portugal Laurels in the long border.

The Honeysuckle, the American Pillar and Breath of Life roses were planted near the fence, they all liked their new home and after 32 years they are still flourishing. A garden changes each season, so by the end of the first year, we were pleased with what we had achieved.

Sadly, in December 1986, Peter the Myna bird died, he was about 15 years old and developed a growth on his vocal chords. We found him at the bottom of his cage. He was buried in the quietest part of the garden, in a corner on the south side, that would never be disturbed.

The house was very quiet without him. The dogs also missed him very much.

Christmas was creeping up on us and nothing had been mentioned about an event for the Senior Citizens, so we asked at church if we could arrange something. There was no objection, so we decided to try an afternoon tea party. We had a coffee morning to raise some money and sent out invitations. The Cub leaders agreed to provide the entertainment. We were delighted that over 40 turned up and it was a very happy afternoon.

An elderly member at church asked if next year we could have a hot meal at lunchtime, so several coffee mornings later to raise funds, we booked the village hall and the cubs, for the week before Christmas. The food was cooked by a number of volunteers, while others made delicious desserts. We had lots of laughter in the entertainment, the cubs all wore top hats (homemade) one little boy's hat kept falling over his face, big brother stood next to him and kept pulling it back up. It was so comical, the audience laughed so much, they were in tears! From then onwards, the Christmas lunches went from strength to strength and numbers doubled! Fortunately, the Senior Citizens Christmas lunch has received funding from the "Leek Nite". The Leek Nite was and still is a small group of villagers, every November they have a competition for the person who has grown the largest leeks! This is held in a pub, they also have an auction and a raffle. The money raised goes to local charities. Every year, from 1989, they have made a generous donation, increasing the amount each year, to cover the cost of the Senior Citizens lunch.

Pat has happy memories at the hospital, when the Salvation Army band went round the wards on Boxing Day. They would arrive about 10.00am in the clinic waiting area, where they could leave their outdoor coats and would spend almost two hours going round the wards, returning to the clinic area for a drink and light refreshments. This had started years ago, when they were playing outside in the rain and they were invited in by the staff.

Led by the Vicar, we joined in singing carols around the village, collecting for Christian Aid.

Castleton has its own old Christmas Carols, which were sung by the lead miners. In 1953, Coronation Year, very few copies existed and the Vicar at that time ventured to print a composite edition of the words and music. In the old days they were sung without music. We were given a copy of the Coronation edition, which helped us master the strange words, which we came to like, when practising with the choir. In Castleton, the carols are sung every year in "The George" and in church.

In 1987 we had a blizzard, the snow ploughs were unable to cope, this was the only time we were unable to travel into work. So we had a Bank

Fun in the snow with Heidi and Toby

Holiday day and enjoyed the snow with the dogs, once the wind abated, we were able to travel to work the following day.

Four years to retirement.

The advent of the Obstetric Theatre and the Special Care Baby Unit made an enormous improvement. The staff, including myself, were all trained to work in the theatre, you never knew who would be on duty when an emergency occurred. From my own point of view, I had always felt that when in charge, you should maintain your skills, in order to take over when required.

My interest was also in supporting mothers with hypertension and stress in pregnancy and I did some research following on from successful work with hypnotherapy by an anaesthetist.

The disadvantages were that it was time consuming, the training of staff was not easy and some mothers were not happy for a therapist having a hold over them. To overcome these disadvantages, over a few months, mothers had been helped using deep relaxation techniques with tape recordings. Initially most of the patients were referred by the medical staff. In particular, they displayed one or more of the following:- Tenseness, Fear, Over Anxiety or Hypertension (high blood pressure). Those patients who were receiving the therapy, were so enthusiastic, that other patients were requesting help. Usually, the patients were counselled individually and taken through at least one session, depending on their needs. They were given a tape to use daily, or whenever they felt the need to relax.

The tapes contained deep relaxation, a pleasant incident, such as a walk down a garden, followed by soothing music. From the research it was apparent that the use of recording tapes was of benefit and reduced the amount of drugs required.

It was at this time that Mary Croft, who had worked in the Maternity Unit for many years and for the last ten years was in charge of the Unit, retired. She was sadly missed by all her staff, who held her in high esteem. Our new boss was very different, I got to the stage of seeking another post, even if it meant downgrading! But she moved elsewhere in less than two years and our new 35 year old boss, was like a breath of fresh air! It was good to spend my last two years happily.

In the later part of 1989, I had yet another one week course to attend, for Supervisors of Midwives, held in Ripon. On the last day at breakfast, a telephone call came for me. It was Muriel to tell me the roof of the barn by the side of our house had been badly damaged by fire. She wanted me to know she was alright in case it was on the news! There were many changes taking place, including shortly, the transfer of Nether Edge Maternity Unit to Northern General Maternity Unit, so before this occurred on 30th September 1990, having worked 40 years in the NHS, I retired 16 months before I could start drawing my pension! I had a marvellous leaving party, with no regrets at making the break!

In finishing my last four years at one go, we will go back to a holiday in

The roof of the barn on fire

Scotland, in June 1987, visiting Machrihanish on the Mull of Kintyre, enjoying the quiet beaches with seals basking in the sun, when the seals barked, the dogs barked back. There were many lovely walks, one day we walked to the Island of Davaar, near Campbell

Our trailer-tent all packed up

Town. You can only walk over the causeway at low tide, there are caves all around the island, in one cave there is a painting on the wall of the Crucifixion, which has been there for over a hundred years, the photograph does not do justice to the colours.

The Crucifiction cave painting

Prince Charles at the opening of the Outdoor centre in Castleton

In 1988 there were major alterations in the church tower, making a first floor which would be the ringing chamber, the ropes had to be shortened, making it safer for the ringers. To reach the chamber we had to negotiate narrow, winding stone steps. On the ground floor level, there would be room for toilet facilities, as well as the refreshment area!

The other things of note at this time, the hand bells were refurbished, very expensive, but well worth it. Muriel was put on the Parochial Church Council.

Pat became Treasurer and booking secretary for the village hall. The Peveril Players had a pantomime, Dick Whittington, we helped with the costumes and the refreshments. Toby swallowed a lamb's tail (the lamb wasn't attached) It took three days to pass through, otherwise all was quiet!

There was great excitement in 1989, when Prince Charles came to open an Outdoor centre, which had been converted from derelict farm buildings. Many from the village including ourselves and the dogs walked over, and the children from the village school. We never expected to get close, but we were on the front row and Prince Charles walked straight over to talk to us. He asked me what sort of dog Toby was and I told him he was a Heinz variety, he looked puzzled and I said 57 varieties, we all burst out laughing.

A few days after this, we were walking in Longshaw (on the moors), there was a small group taking photographs, a lady ran over to us and asked if they could borrow the dog for a photograph. It was Toby they wanted because he was white and a bit of black. They were from 'Next' preparing for their new catalogue. It took quite a time, taking all the pictures. Toby would have had Heidi with him, but they only wanted one dog! We did get a catalogue showing Toby performing!

Heidi was now over 14 years old and she had what was thought to be a heart attack or a mild stroke. She was put on tablets twice daily and she responded well.

It was in late 1988 that we became vegetarians, we had over the past two years reduced our meat intake, occasionally having fish. The reason was, that the cattle were given hormones, which we disagreed with. A few years later, we talked to a farmer, who had previously been a vet, he said he hung his head in shame, when he thought of all the hormone implants he was asked to do and it was wrong.

Soon after this, with the reported amount of cruelty to animals, we became completely vegetarian.

Both of us joined the local branch of the W.I., which we enjoyed very much, particularly the regular long walks, visiting areas we had not visited before, there were usually up to about 20 in the group.

We were both competitive, entering all the competitions, in the Horticultural sections at Hope Show and Bakewell Show, we were delighted with all our successes. The W.I. had a large Marquee at the Bakewell Show and as well as individual entries, there were larger displays, where perhaps four could do a joint effort, for example, arranging and providing a meal which was judged and I remember coming either first or second on one occasion. The standard was always very high.

Muriel with Heidi and Toby

After Pat's retirement, she started going to Decoupage classes at the College. She made many pictures using the intricate 3'D' method and I sold several of them at a Royal College of Midwives meeting. I also made one for our cousins as a wedding present. My first small picture, I kept and it is on the wall in my bedroom.

Heidi who followed us home from Ecclesall Woods, only a puppy

Muriel's main hobby was and still is, gardening, she is also a keen knitter. She has made a beautiful intricate bedspread, which won her a prize. She has also made numerous toys.

It was in October 1990 that Heidi died, over 15 years old. She had given us so much pleasure. We both missed her very much and Toby was devastated, wandering around looking for her.

In 1991 we held a very successful Church Festival, the theme was our Patron Saint, St. Edmund. We wrote to 60 churches who had the same Patron Saint and we received some fascinating information which we were able to use. On the Sunday evening we held a 'Songs of Praise' in the marketplace with Castleton Silver Band and a guitarist, providing the musical accompaniment.

The Village Hall had to raise £10,000 for a new floor, so Pat as secretary and treasurer was involved in organising a Club lottery, which would raise a substantial amount. The Peveril Players held a pantomime - Robin Hood - with the profits going towards the new floor.

It was the year, just before Christmas, when we had severe flooding. Following several days and nights of hard frosts, we then had torrential rain, the rivers overflowed their banks. One felt helpless watching the water rising, filling more and more sandbags! Our porch and garage were flooded, but some cottages were much worse than us. There was eventually a lot of preventative work undertaken in the village to improve the drainage, which has so far successfully rectified the problem of flooding.

Pat as the Genie in Aladdin tap dancing

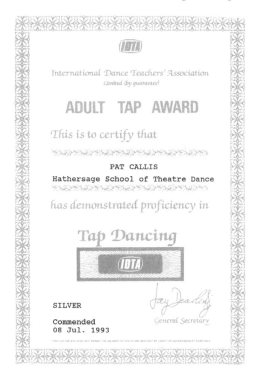

International Dance Teachers' Association
Limited (by guarantee)

ADULT TAP AWARD

This is to certify that

PAT CALLIS
Hathersage School of Theatre Dance

has demonstrated proficiency in

Tap Dancing

SILVER

Commended
08 Jul. 1993

General Secretary

Tap dancing was popular at this time and a dancing teacher held classes in Hathersage, Pat decided it would be good exercise. It was great fun and we even got to the stage of taking the bronze exam, the 'Adult Tappers' did a turn at the dancing class concert. A year later, gaining a Silver medal, we performed two items in the next concert. The classes came to an abrupt halt when our teacher's husband had a bad accident. I had really enjoyed it while it lasted.

In 1992 we had a new neighbour, Kath Haddock who moved from a larger house in the village. She was a lovely lady who was anxious to participate in all our activities. In particular, she was keen to be involved with hand bell ringing, Both Muriel and I had practiced playing 'four in hand', you have two bells in each hand and we needed someone to play four more bells, Kath rang off the table using slightly heavier bells, very soon she became expert!

The April of the same year saw the start of the W.I. Market! It was held in the 'Little John' at Hathersage every Friday morning, so Thursday became a cooking day! The regular fare we made were breadcakes, teacakes, pizzas, carrot cakes, vegetarian savoury dishes and jar upon jar of marmalade and chutney. Muriel sold numerous plants and we both made toys for sale, she was still working at the dental practice 15 hours a week and hoped to reduce to 12 hours soon.

Retirement became a bit of a joke, we were busier than ever! But we also had lots of fun, particularly in March 1993, when we had a village pantomime – Aladdin. Pat was the 'Mummy', completely

The full cast

At Marila and Neil's wedding in Blackpool

wrapped in white bandages from head to toe, on stage with the wicked Abanazar at the start of the performance. She then had the part of the 'Genie of the Lamp'. Muriel was front of house, plus a walking on part. The cave scene was spectacular, the Genie's entry was perfectly timed, with a flash, a cloud of smoke and then the cave was lit up. The Genie also performed a tap dance to fill in a passage of time. The Peveril Players did an amazing job with the scenery, costumes and the band making it a very professional show. The next year, there was a 'Follies' in December, when we played the Can-Can on the hand bells.

We had a pleasant surprise when we received an invitation to our cousin's daughter's wedding which we were delighted to accept. This was on Saturday 12th June 1993, 1.00pm at St. Paul's Church, Marton, Blackpool. We drove to Blackpool on a sunny day arriving in good time, of course Toby was invited, as an honoured guest! Marila looked lovely, she and Neil made a great pair and we enjoyed being part of the day. The hotel for the reception was on the sea front and we had been able to book a room to stay the night.

In 1993 we joined a two year course for the Bishop's Certificate in Christian Studies. There were seven of us on the course, led by a Curate, Ethel Milroy at Tideswell Church. We met for six sessions each term, also three study days per year at Breadsall, near Derby.

We also had to undertake projects, such as Christian response to social issues, Celebration of Creativity, My Spiritual Journey were examples. The skills we had for the course were in entertaining, cooking, hand bell ringing, needlework and other hand crafts. On the course we had to produce written work on the sessions including the study days we had to attend. Due to the commitment that was required, we decided that we would resign from the Choir, but continue with developing our Tower Bell skills.

Our first skills were involved with cooking and charitable work. The skill to raise money was involved, we decided that we would use our own home and garden for all events as an 'open house', this would save hiring expenses.

The High Peak Hospice was providing day care in a house on the outskirts of Chapel-en-le-Frith particularly for cancer sufferers. A friend in the village was a client at the hospice and she said that the facilities for the work they were doing, were very sparse. She suggested that if we could provide a carpet and some curtains it would be a start.

We decided to hold a bring and buy sale, plant stall, raffle and offer lunches and teas. We had a vegetarian menu with a choice of three dishes for lunch:- Lasagne and Peas, Savoury Pie and Peas or Quiche and Salad, followed by fresh Fruit Salad and Cream plus Coffee for a minimum donation of £2. The Tea was homemade bread roll with a choice of fillings, scones with blackcurrant jelly and a variety of cakes for a minimum donation of £1. We served 60 meals in relays of 20, with the help of two neighbours and around 30 came for tea. Our neighbour Kath served on the stall and another neighbour did the raffle. We made an amazing £654.00!

Just seven weeks later, there was a plea for 'Hope for Romania', so on the 13th November 1993 we held a Coffee Morning, followed by a choice of four homemade soups, Ploughman's lunch and coffee for a minimum donation of £1.50. We realised that very few came for coffee, but came a little later for lunch. We raised £350.00, the money going to purchase a list of urgently needed drugs.

Our good friend David Fox, who drove the van to Romania, had received many donations and we were able to help him purchase medical equipment, which included Nebulisers, Sphygmomanometers, Stethoscopes and a Fibre Optic Ophthalmoscope. It was gratifying to hear on David's return, that an Eye Specialist had just commenced work at the hospital with barely any equipment, so our supplies were cherished – we felt the Lord had guided us.

'Hope for Romania' was now high on our list. Our house quickly began to look like a Medical Warehouse, all had to be checked as they arrived. We needed to do more, so we put out notices for March 26th 1994, inviting people to a pre-

INVOICE

The Humanitarian Relief Foundation
Registered Charity No. 1701
c/o 20 Florence Avenue
Aston
Sheffield S31 0RL   Tax Point 310595

5	500	Amitriptyline 10mg tabs	8.50
5	500	Amitriptyline 25mg tabs	8.00
5	100	Amitriptyline 50mg tabs	12.75
40	100ml	Amoxycillin syrup 125mg/5ml	26.20
4	500	Amoxycillin 250mg caps	50.00
10	120	Cimetidine 200mg tabs	25.50
20	60	Cimetidine 400mg tabs	48.00
20	100ml	Co-Trimoxazole paediatric suspension	11.00
2	500	Co-Trimoxazole 480mg tabs	15.00
5	1000	Diazepam 2mg tabs	8.75
5	1000	Diazepam 5mg tabs	9.50
5	500	Diazepam 10mg tabs	8.50
5	100	Diclofenac 25mg tabs	6.00
5	100	Diclofenac 50mg tabs	8.25
2	500	Erythromycin 250mg tabs	30.50
20	100ml	Erythromycin 125mg/5ml susp.	15.80
20	100ml	Erythromycin 250mg/5ml susp.	25.00
4	500	Ibuprofen 200mg tabs	11.00
5	250	Ibuprofen 400mg tabs	13.50
3	500	Metoclopramide 10mg tabs	5.25
8	100	Naproxen 500mg tabs	58.00
1	1000	Oxytetracycline 250mg tabs	8.75
2	5000	Paracetamol 500mg tabs	33.20
50	1	Salbutamol inhalers	59.00

TOTAL	503.95
less adjustment	- 3.95
NETT	500.00
VAT - ZERO RATED - CHARITABLE DONATION	0.00
NOW DUE	500.00

J. STEPHEN HAWKINS LTD.
HAWKINS PHARMACY
149 BURNGREAVE RD.,
SHEFFIELD, S3 9DL
Tel. (0114) 275-4920

Received = thanks 2/6/95

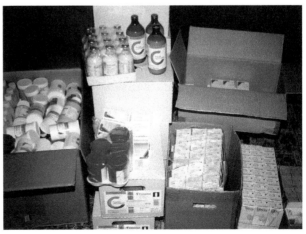

The goods were delivered to our house
ready for David to collect

booked lunch, with three sittings 12noon, 12.45pm and 1.30pm with a menu of Savoury pie, Lasagne or Potato & Leek Gratin, followed by Fruit Salad or Bakewell Tart or Lemon Sponge. We asked for a minimum of £2.50 for the meal, coffee and mints were served in the lounge where there was also a cake/cookie stall. We raised £450.00, of which £350 for drugs and for Easter £100.00 was used on food items and some Easter eggs for the children in an orphanage.

The last big event for Romania came in response to a telephone call from David saying he would be making another journey at Easter 1995, please could we do anything to help?

A lunch was the obvious choice – as we are both vegetarian and the meals so far had been vegetarian, without drawing to it, so we decided to suggest they should 'Savour the delights of a vegetarian lunch'! The menu:- Leek & Aduki Bean Casserole with Cheese potato, Vegetable Gratin with Rosemary Crumble topping, Savoury Pie & Peas. Desserts:-Fruit Salad & Cream, Sherry Trifle or Cheese & Biscuits.

The date was set for Saturday 26th February 1995. We decided to have four sittings! Bookings were slow, had we picked the wrong day or were they put off by the menu? Sure enough, the numbers increased to 50, then 60 and in the last few days the telephone was non-stop. The final figure was 87, which included six 'takeaways'. The minimum donation for the meal was £2.50.

Although many locals came, there were visitors from a wide area, including Bradwell, Grindleford, Calver, Hathersage, Bamford, Monyash, Sheffield and Dronfield.

The atmosphere at the lunch was marvellous, with our neighbours doing a great job helping with the serving and washing up! Kath was in charge of a stall, which was a 'sell out'.

Our last visitors left at 3.00pm and we eagerly counted the proceeds, which amounted to £500.00! The total raised for Romania in the two years was £1,300.00. We received a lovely thank you letter from the Doctors in Romania.

The second event for High Peak Hospice consisted of two Organic Gardening weekends in June and August 1994. Muriel undertook tours of the garden, explaining how organic methods worked, whilst Pat provided teas and Kath was on the produce stall. About 70 came to the first weekend and around 100 to the second. The three events we staged for the Hospice raised £1,084.71. We received a lovely thank you letter after each event.

The Plight of Rwanda was shown on Television in August

MEDICAL CENTER
BETANIA
S.R.L.

Dr. IOAN CREȚ , Dr. LIVIA CREȚ
3700 ORADEA , ROMÂNIA , Str. Menumorut 12 ap. 1 , Tel.:059 / 164836

Dear

Pat & Muriel
Callis

Greetings from ORADEA, Romania.

First of all we would like to thank you very much for your donation (medicine) to our christian MEDICAL CENTER.
It's a big blessing for us to have friends in England who don't forget our needs.
We would like to tell you that all medicines wich you put us are very helpfull in our medical activity, first of all antibiotics & pain killers.
The medicines are distributed free for patients (adults & children), in accordance with diagnostic; a percent of these patients are very poor and it's a big blessing for them to obtain these free.
May God bless you in your activity and if you would like to visit Romania you are well come in our medical center.

Sincerely
John & Livia
CREȚ

ORADEA, 16.JUNE 1995

1994, we decided that the items the two of us made and sold on the W.I. stall at the local Hope Show would be donated to the appeal. This amounted to £50.00, but the following morning we listened to the Radio 4 morning service given by the Salvation Army, there was a direct telephone link to their Army Officer in Rwanda. He spoke of the problems there and the need for an orphanage. The service made such an impression on us that we decided to donate £100.00 to this appeal. We received a very nice acknowledgement.

Also in February 1994, the Archbishop of Canterbury, who had recently been to the Sudan and witnessed the terrible suffering among the people, after years of war, hunger and persecution. We decided to have a 'Hunger Lunch' and contacted the local churches, including the Roman Catholic Church, asking for their support.

Posters were placed on all the notice boards inviting everyone to come on Sunday 20th to our house between 11.45am and 2.15pm to share a simple meal. Three types of soup were made with bread rolls, cheese, fresh fruit and coffee. At least 50 people came for a meal and others made donations.

The friendship was most gratifying and we received delightful letters from Archbishop George for the gift of £268.00 and one from the Roman Catholic Priest, Peter Moran, saying how much he had enjoyed it.

Hand bell ringing to raise money for Save the Children

The two of us plus our neighbour Kath, practiced with hand bells every Monday afternoon and throughout the two years of undertaking the Bishop's Certificate, we entertained numerous Friendship Clubs and Rest/Nursing Homes. Although we never asked for donations, we were often given a small gift. In the two years this amounted to £35 which we donated to Christian Aid.

During the Christmas Period, we visited all the local pubs and restaurants, making a collection for 'Save the Children'. In 1993 we were able to send £240.00 and in 1994, the 75th Anniversary of Save the Children – £325.00.

Our last effort was to raise money for a Sound Reinforcement and Loop System in the Village Hall. On April 24th 1995 with the help of the Friendship Club, we had a Coffee Morning, Bring & Buy, Raffle and Soup & Roll Lunch in the village hall, raising £338.00. The total raised between September 1993 and June 1995 was £3,690.71.

The other element of the Bishop's Certificate which took up any spare time was stitching the Tapestry, for the creativity part. We had ordered a double kneeler for use at weddings for the bride and groom to kneel on during the service. It was quite a time consuming job, which had to be completed within the two years!

We required one more objective bringing in a social activity. From a recent village appraisal, it had shown that the 50 plus age group needed a daytime group activity, this would be an ideal project for us to be involved in.

The birth of the Friendship Club was on January 10th in the Village Hall. We had publicised this with posters, in the Parish Magazine, at the Christmas Lunch, in the local shops, the Doctor's surgery (the surgery was in the village at this time) and by word of mouth. Three friends joined us to lead the meeting and to our surprise 35 potential members came. We explained our suggestions and then gave out paper and pencils for everyone to write down their ideas, over a cup of tea or coffee. The suggestions included indoor bowls, dominoes, card games, flower arranging, darts, Scrabble and outings.

It was decided that the meetings would be on the 2nd and 4th Wednesdays of each month 2.00pm to 3.30pm, a charge of 30 pence per meeting, which would include a small raffle prize, a cup of tea or coffee and a biscuit. A committee was formed and it was good that of the seven members, there were two gentlemen. The members decided they would be known as Castleton Friendship Club and a bank account was opened in that name. A typical afternoon, after greeting members who paid their sub on entry, commenced with simple limbering up exercises to taped music with Pauline in charge of the squeaky neck, joints, arms and legs, then whilst we were all together, notices were given, before we dispersed to the activity of our preference.

Outings were also very popular in the summer months, visiting different beauty spots in Derbyshire. The club flourished with an average number of 30. We both enjoyed the different study days on the Bishop's Certificate Course and particularly spending a weekend at Morley, a retreat house in Derbyshire. The Warden kindly allowed us to camp in the orchard enabling us to take our aging dog Toby with us. The theme was 'All are called' with Francis Dewar who had written books, leading the weekend, which was truly unforgettable.

Our two year course was coming to an end, we had completed all the items we had promised and our course leader and mentor were both happy with all we had achieved for the Bishop's Centre of Learning. We received an invitation to be present at the Presentation of

Presentation of the Bishop's Certificates awards at Derby Catherdral. Pat and Muriel are second row, second and third on the right

Certificates on Friday 27th October1995 in Derby Cathedral.

The Presentation was at 7.30pm, but we had been asked to display the projects we had undertaken and there was a special area to place them, so people could see them.

Our back garden taking shape!

The service took place in the retrochoir followed by a light buffet, tea or coffee, in the chapter room. It was a lovely evening and we were called up individually to receive our certificates. I knew the Bishop and his wife when they lived in Sheffield and they both came to my preparation for childbirth classes and he announced this when I received my certificate! The photograph was taken of the whole group.

The Garden - 10 Years on.

Muriel now gives a short interlude to tell you about the alterations to the garden. In 1995 we felt we should do something about the driveway, following a dry summer, the grass down the centre of the drive had sunk making it uneven. Also the flash flooding in July, formed a moat round the bungalow, so the drainage needed improving. In August we visited the Bakewell Show, we saw a firm demonstrating a different method of paving and thought it would be ideal for us. We placed our order and the work would commence in 6 to 8 weeks. The higher stone wall round the house, holding back the soil had all been completed.

A lot of preparatory work was required, before the concrete arrived. It was very exciting watching it happen, the surface is reinforced concrete which is imprinted with a pattern to make a cobbled effect and left overnight for the concrete to dry. A seal was painted on with brushes and left for the drying process to be completed.

They allowed for expansion which included a 'French Drain' around two sides of the stone wall.

The drive was much admired and it still looks almost as good 20 years later, with only the odd crack. Expensive, but well worth it. The laurel tree near the front fence developed an infection and had to be removed to prevent it contaminating the other one, which is a good sanctuary for the birds. We started putting perennial plants in to cover the flowering season, winter heathers like our soil. We tend to keep off plants which the slugs like.

We now have three apple trees behind the garage with the raspberry canes, summer and autumn ones which enable us to make seedless jam which has a ready sale. We take cuttings off many plants which increases our stock at no extra cost.

We had a lovely present of a garden seat from friends who were related to our late neighbours in Sheffield, as a 'thank you' for looking after them.

In the same year we had a new kitchen fitted in March, it had got desperate when a drawer kept falling apart and ' araldite' doesn't last for ever! We changed to two electric ovens, one a fan oven and a smaller traditional one, which we preferred. It was so much easier with all the cooking!

The Peveril Players decided to perform Noel Coward's play 'Blithe Spirit' in May. Pat was given the part of the Doctor's Wife, which ended up with a 'Toy Boy' as the Doctor! They had to age him 40 years which was simpler than making me look younger! We had super 'write ups'.

We also needed a peaceful holiday, so we had a week on the canal. We hired a super 60 foot narrow boat (on a special offer) from Acton Bridge travelling along the Trent, Mersey and the Shropshire Union Canal as far as Chester.

The later part of the year was preparing for our big event, in May 1996, which was in aid of roof repairs and refurbishment in St Edmund's Church.

We had all the organising to undertake mobilising everyone who would be able to help in this mammoth task. The main part centred on a Flower Festival in Church, the theme being 'Sunshine and Shadows'.

The Festival was for eight days and our aims were threefold – Village Unity, Evangelism and to raise money for the appeal. We wanted to give emphasis to the younger age group, so a Children's Art competition depicting the theme, which would have to be well advertised. Then we considered a tape, with the children of the Hope Valley Schools singing and we could sell the tapes. At a previous event we had met the Rev. Roly Bain, Anglican Minister and Professional Clown, who brought Christianity through Clowning, he was the Grandson of the 'Romany' of Children's hour fame in the 1940's. We wrote to ask if he could spend two days in Castleton.
For all this to come to fruition it would be expensive, but as the saying goes 'you have to speculate to accumulate'!

We wrote to over 20 establishments in the area, asking for sponsorship and the response was amazing. We also wanted a well-known person to come to the opening and started writing with details of our church and what we were trying to achieve. Those we contacted were Wendy Craig, Kathy Staff, the BBC, Pam Rhodes, Thelma Barlow and Terry Waite. We had lovely personal replies from them all, we still have the letters, but for various reasons they were unable to accept our invitation. We asked around and someone suggested Pollyanna Pickering, the famous Wildlife Artist who lived in Derbyshire.

This was a brilliant suggestion, bearing in mind that we could ask if she would also present the prizes for the Children's Art competition. We received a reply that she would be delighted to come.

Looking for ideas depicting one of the arrangements, we found a poem by David Kossoff, so we wrote to him asking for permission to use it. We had a most delightful letter saying, 'Of course you may use the words'. He also enclosed details of a performance he could do in church, if it would be feasible, it could also raise money.

Everyone agreed and we wrote back to thank him for agreeing to the words and we would be thrilled to have a performance. This would take place on Saturday 11th May 7.30pm in Church. We made a booking for him and his assistant at the Nag's Head Hotel. In a further letter, he confirmed his simple staging needs and offered further material for making the programmes/tickets, which could be reproduced and enlarged. The performance would be 90 minutes and had no interval. The Rev. Roly Bain also replied that he would be able to spend two days with us and he was booked in at the Peak Hotel. We were very grateful to the hotels for their generosity.

The Art Competition was creating a lot of interest, so we booked the Village Hall from Friday and over the first weekend to display the entries.

For the tape of the children singing, the headteachers at all the schools welcomed us and we had a local friend, Paul, who undertook to do the recordings. A special award was made for the best design for the audio tape sleeve.

Our last major task was to organise the floral arrangements in Church. We were both members of the Association of Church of England Flower Arrangers, so we had some contacts and other friends who were all excellent Flower Arrangers, but they would need time to decide how they would interpret their arrangement and the type of flowers that would be most suitable. We visited all of them and they were all thrilled to be asked!

As we had done most of the spadework, we decided to have a March holiday, to recharge our batteries, for the final organisation of the Festival.

Muriel on the right, Llangollen canal

We also realised that for many reasons, this may be our last canal holiday. Bearing this in mind, we decided that we would write a little at this stage about our canal experiences, before we continue with the festival.

Over the years we have been on many canals, a popular one is the Llangollen. In 1996 we chose this canal, as it was a favourite. The first time you cross the famous viaduct it can be scary, the narrow channel being so high above the River Dee. The canal into Llangollen is also narrow and often lacking in water and difficult if you have to pass a large narrow boat. On another occasion, we hired a boat from Whalley Bridge mooring for the night, at the end of the Whalley arm and took the dog for a walk, on returning we were shattered to see the boat floating in the middle of the canal, some youths had untied our mooring rope, fortunately we could grasp the rope and pull the boat in, it was

105

Pulling the boat in

the only time we had a boat tampered with. On the same trip we went though Manchester, going down the 'Rochdale nine', the locks then, were in very poor condition and the water flowed through like Niagra Falls! Due to a lack of time we had to come back the same way, quite an experience! Another time we had moored for the night to be awakened at 6.00am and told if we didn't move soon we would be stuck there as they were closing that section of the canal! The Oxford Canal is quite different, it is flat, so you don't have many locks, but there are swing and lift bridges. We found the Birmingham Canal interesting and there are plenty of locks. Canals have been exciting for us, you never knew what would be round the next corner. It is like going back in time, you are in a different world, yet meeting many like minded friendly people.

On our return we had eight weeks to make sure everything was done! There were posters, programmes and tickets for two evening events to have printed, prizes for the competition to buy. We had to confirm the dates and

Presentation of the winners of the Children's Act competition

times with the ten organists from different churches in a wide area, the hand bell ringers, visiting tower bell ringers and our local school, who were all going to provide entertainment in the afternoons.

The Children's Art competition had 200 entries, the three judges Lyn, Sonya and Joyce made some excellent decisions.

Three friends, Barbara, Sheila and Pauline volunteered to display the artwork for us in the Village Hall, which was an immense weight off our shoulders. The tapes with the children singing were made and went on sale in the village hall. The opening day arrived, all the hard work by so many people was completed and the church looked fantastic and the village hall beautifully set out with the children's pictures. The Flower Arrangers work was much admired, the book which people signed, was full of praise. Prompt at 10.30am, there was a short service for the opening ceremony, with a welcome by the Vicar, Michael Collier followed by the hymn 'This is the day'. After the flower arrangers prayer. Pollyanna Pickering officially opened the Festival, followed by the final happy hymn 'Shine, Jesus, Shine'. We then retired to the Village Hall, where the prizes were presented by our opener who was delightful talking to all the children as they came up for their prize. The overall winner was 8 year old Anne Talbot from Hope, her picture was lovely. The volunteers for refreshments had a busy time both in church and in the Village Hall, throughout the eight days.

On the first Saturday evening, David Kossoff gave a memorable 90 minute performance of 'As according to Kossoff' to a full audience in church. Followed by a finger buffet across the road from church, at Cryer House, where his book could be purchased.

David Kossoff and his assistant Pam were delightful and so easy to talk to. They were very interested in the caverns in Castleton, so on the Sunday morning Pat took them round one of the caverns which they thoroughly enjoyed. We received two lovely personal handwritten letters from him saying how much they had enjoyed their weekend in Castleton. The week was very successful, with the organ recitals, the schoolchildren's singing, and hand bell and tower bell ringers attracting large audiences.

On the Wednesday and Thursday the village welcomed Rev. Roly Bain, Anglican Minister and Professional Clown. Roly, on both days, he visited schools in the valley, bringing fun and laughter to the children, while in everything he did or said delivering a Christian message.

His visit coincided with an Ascension Day Service on the Thursday night and with the children dressed as clowns. His clowning gave us all the perfect Ascension story. Finally, the children and adults wrote names of people and other things, to be prayed for, on helium filled balloons, then we all went outside and let them go into the sky, as visible prayers from us all, again, so appropriate for Ascension day.

The culmination of the Festival on Sunday night should have been a torchlight procession to Peveril Castle for 'Song of Praise' with the Castleton

Rev. Roly Bain, Anglican Minister and professional clown at the village school, bringing fun and laughter

Silver Band, but the heavens opened, so we all diverted to the Castleton Youth Hostel where the band played and we all sang with great enthusiasm.

Our three aims of the Festival were fulfilled. Unity in the villages and beyond, Evangelism with all the events and the help from David and Roly, thirdly the amount raised for the Restoration Appeal was £4,060.46!

Sadly on the 7th June Toby died. He was 13 and a half years old and had been such a good friend and he worshipped us. We missed him so much, but decided to wait a while before having another dog.

Toby in his youth

Following the Festival there were two National Organic Gardening weekends, June 22nd and 23rd and August 3rd and 4th. In the middle of getting ready for these two weekends, we had a lovely surprise in the post. The insurance policy we had been paying into for many years had matured and the amount was sufficient for us to visit Canada and America. Our Mother had lived there before and during the first World War, she had been engaged to a Canadian boy who was in the forces and was sent to France. He was wounded and died, the letters sent to Mother from the field hospital, had been kept in a box and it had always been our wish to take them to the War Museum in Ottawa, here was our chance, so with the help of Gillian at Thomas Cook, we set the wheels in motion for five weeks, commencing Sepember15th, for a 'trip of a lifetime'. More about this later, before then we had commitments, which had to be fulfilled. The first was the two Organic Gardening Weekends, for these we had to do quite a lot of work in the garden, as well as preparing lunches and teas, stalls with goodies and plants for sale. At these events, Muriel was involved in talking to visitors about organic methods, whilst Pat and helpers provided the food. We were blessed on each occasion with fine weather and the two weekends raised £750.00 for local charities, one being the local school, we also sent £80.00 to the 'Henry Doubleday Organic Research Unit.

We had become Life Members of Hope Valley Horticultural Show, which held an Annual Show each Bank Holiday, at the end of August, which attracts hundreds of farmers and visitors from far and wide. It was a full day out! In particular, our interest was the Horticultural competition tent, this had all types of vegetables, flowers, flower arrangements, home cooking, jams, preserves, eggs, a craft section and a children's section. The judging was very keen and it was very competitive. Any goods left over, were auctioned off at the end. Muriel did take over as Secretary and Pat for many years, acted as Auctioneer. Many of the villages had their own Horticultural Society, but not Castleton, so we had joined the Hope group.

The events were held in Loxley Hall, Hope, a show had been arranged on Saturday 14th September. This meant a full day putting the tables out, labelling them ready for the entries, to be received by 10.30am, the judging starting at 11.00am, sorting out the winners, then it was open to the public from 2.00pm. By 5.00pm after the prizes had been given out, it was a case of putting the room in order. All this the day before our five weeks holiday!

A journey of about 12,000miles.

On Sunday 15th September we left Castleton Bus station at 12noon to catch the 1.20pm train to London. Thomas Cook had booked First Class seats for us, which included free coffee. In London we took the Piccadilly Line to Heathrow Airport – it was crowded!, then by courtesy bus, arriving at the Ibis Hotel at 7.00pm. We ate our tea watching Treasure Hunt and Pie in the Sky, although we were apt to nod off! On Monday, we woke bright and early at 6.00am ready for the great day, after breakfast and a walk round the block, the coach took us to Terminal 3 for 9.40am. It was the first time Muriel had flown and only Pat's second time. The Thomas Cook representatives speedily assisted us through the formalities. All the passengers flying Air Canada were given a badge to commemorate 50 years of flying from England to Canada and vice versa. The plane 50 years ago was a Lancaster and the crossing took 20 hours. Our flying time now in a Boeing 767 would only take six and a half hours.

Take off was delayed due to a baggage problem, whilst waiting we saw Concorde leave. We had window seats and at a height of 25,000 feet we could identify the Bristol Channel, the South Wales coast, Irish Sea and Ireland. We were served drinks, and as we were vegetarians, we were served lunch first! We passed time above the clouds, knitting teddy bears, ready for the Christmas market. The clocks had to be advanced six hours, so we had lunch at 2.30pm and tea at 2.00pm. It was fine when we flew up the St. Lawrence Waterway, but the pilot warned us the weather in Montreal was heavy cloud and rain! This was so at Mirabel Airport, the bus journey to the hotel took about 45 minutes.

The hotel was very pleasant and we had the luxury of a double bed each! For those who haven't been to Canada, you could walk straight into a shopping mall, three floors and you can continue walking underground all day, if you wanted to, which is ideal for the Canadian winters. We had never seen so many restaurants, eating out was the done thing.

The following day at 9.00am, we had a bus tour of Montreal, our guide Peter, known as St. Peter, who was a real joker, showed us all the different areas, including the Botanical Gardens and the Olympic Stadium, arriving back at 11.45am. The rest of the day was free to do what we wanted, we had a meal and walked to Old Montreal and the docklands. The Hotel Concierge advised us where to find a mini-market, where we could buy food to have in our room.

The next morning, our bags packed, we were free until midday, so we went a short train ride to the Olympic Stadium and Botanical Gardens, which was interesting and you could take a 'run-about' to the greenhouses. Back at the hotel we boarded the coach to take us to Ottawa. After booking in at the Lord Elgin Hotel, we returned to our coach for a tour of the city. Louise was our guide showing us the Parliament building, the Centennial flame, sculptures of the past Prime Ministers and Queen Elizabeth on horseback. We crossed over Portage Bridge to the Museum of Civilisation, the Governor General's house, the Prime Minister's house, Rideau Falls, Byward Market, arriving back at the hotel at 5.30pm. We had a meal in the Rideau Centre, but we really had to search for vegetarian food. Then, walking through the mall, we found a supermarket to buy food for breakfast. It was easier to have breakfast in our room. We also contacted a cousin, Peggy, and arranged to meet her. Louise had warned us to be early if we wanted to go inside the Parliament Buildings, so the next morning we arrived at 8.50am, we joined the queue and went through the x-ray entrance, only to find we were in a Spanish party, the English tour was at 9.20am, but they let us sit down and wait, giving us the opportunity to watch a video of Parliament. On the tour we saw the Speaker's procession, he said 'good morning' and hoped we would enjoy our visit.

Statue at the entrance to the Museum of Civilisation
- Children holding an apple

You were allowed to go in the Visitor's Gallery, following another x-ray check and leaving your coat and camera in a special area. We watched proceedings from the Gallery. Our next visit was to the War Museum, to take the two field hospital letters from the 1st World War, Gordon had been seriously wounded at Passchendaele, dying of his injuries. The staff were delighted to receive them, we later received a letter thanking us with other details of the museum.

We then went to the Museum of Civilisation, where Canadian History is traced from the Indians to modern day, it was an amazing museum, we really needed much longer to take everything in, but we had an appointment to meet Peggy!

The road to her apartment, followed the Ottawa River, the countryside was very attractive. Although she lived by herself she had two large freezers, a large refrigerator, and large oven, they obviously have to prepare for a hard winter. We had a meal together, and got back to the hotel at 8.30pm. After an early breakfast we went to see the Byward Market, where the farmers bring their produce for sale. We bought apples and peaches, then went back to the hotel for our cases, for the next part of our journey at 8.30am, to take us to Toronto. It was a pleasant morning and we had several stops, the first was at Angelo's for coffee, it was a favourite stop for the truck drivers, we were able to have a good look at the trucks and talk to the drivers. We later stopped at Halsteads Bay, overlooking Lake Ontario, then on to Kingston for lunch. The countryside was then rather flat, so Rosa, our courier, took the opportunity to show a video about the River Rafting experience, we would have the opportunity do this later on the tour. The next stop was 'The Big Apple' you could watch the cooks making all types of apple dishes, which you could buy or sample in the restaurant, they were very good!

The highway into Toronto became wider and busier with up to ten lanes of traffic, it was a much larger and more expensive city very fast and busy. The Holiday Inn, where we stayed, had lovely rooms, we were on the 12th floor, with views over the city, but so busy. The squirrels crossed the road by going up the telephone pole, across the wires and down the other side! At 9.00am the following day, we boarded the coach for a tour of the city.

John Cunningham our driver and guide, called out the buildings, some were named after famous people, Glass and Gold featured in some buildings, we passed the Farmers Market and Market Hall, to the CN Tower which is 447 metres high, two observation levels, one inside and one outside. Part of the lower level has a glass floor, through which, far, far below you could see the football stadium, it was eerie walking on it. Our tour continued through the dock area and the Military base with a Lancaster on display. Nearby the area is known as Little Norway, it was here that the Norwegian Air Force came to

practice, whilst Norway was occupied by the Germans in the Second World War and a park contains statues similar to Oslo's Weigland Park. Then, on to the shopping areas, Etams and the world's largest bookstore, then the University, arriving back at the hotel at 12.45pm. After lunch in a nearby restaurant, we went back to the hotel and packed a picnic and went down to the harbour, to catch a ferry to take us to the ' Three Islands', which are a complete contrast to Toronto, you feel as though you are in a 'time warp' it is so quiet and peaceful. An Island girl was being married in the little church, it was charming watching her. We had a drink at the restaurant, ate our picnic and returned back to the mainland on the 7.00pm ferry.

On Sunday 22nd September, we had a day trip to Niagara, the weather was dull and drizzly. We drove along Queen Mary Highway, crossing the Welland Canal, which had eight locks, there used to be 40 locks, raising the canal 40 feet, the canal is between Lake Erie and Lake Ontario. On arrival at the Falls, we went to the pier, to board 'Maid of the Mist', this was the first boat, which was lucky, as there were crowds of people. We went on the top deck, shrouded in blue plastic capes. The water was turbulent, the spray and roar of the water was unbelievable. There must have been several hundred people on each boat, the boats go right under the 'Falls', photography is impossible, you get very wet! It is a fantastic, frightening experience and all too soon it's over, the boat returning to the pier.

Our boat going under the Niagra Falls

We went to the Gift shop and walked to the gardens, to the hotel for lunch in the Penthouse Suite overlooking the Falls.

There are many stories of 'The Maid of the Mist', an Indian Princess was to be married, but was unsure of her future husband. She set off in a boat to meet him, but the God of Thundering Waters intercepted and took her to live with him in the mist of the Falls. We parked at a view point and walked through a park, there were greenhouses with humming birds and other exotic birds flying to and fro. The Falls end in the gorge and flows into a river. From there we went to the town of Niagara on the lake, a delightful township, modern, yet retaining a quaintness. One shop, Greaves, sold homemade jams and marmalades and so back to Toronto for our last evening there.

At 8.30am, on a brilliant sunny day, we went by coach to Toronto Airport, boarding a Boeing 767 to take us over the prairies to Calgary. On landing, our coach was waiting with our driver and guide, Isabel. Calgary had fewer high buildings and less traffic, enroute she showed us the buffalo jumps of years ago, erected to slow the animals down, so that they could be speared or killed with an arrow, to provide meat for the winter.

It was a beautiful area, with green fir trees going up the mountains, the Rockies in the background, with snow on the summits. We arrived at Banff, driving through the town to Sulphur Mountain, where with 20 of our party, took a gondola ride up the mountain. The views were superb, with the brilliant sunshine on the snow-capped mountains.

There was a restaurant and gift shop at the summit, we then returned to the gondola, for our journey down and our coach took us to the Travellers Inn. The rooms were chalet style, unfortunately, one of our suitcases was missing, it was found at Calgary Airport and dispatched to the hotel with an apology from Air Canada. We went to the shops and found a Safeway store, where we were able to buy food for tea and breakfast. The next day we went on one of the optional tours, for a day in the mountains. Our first stop was Johnston Canyon, a walk to the lower falls, which were glacial, the water in the canyon was crystal clear. Our next stop was Moraine Lake, we had to climb up a rocky path to reach the lake, the road is closed during the winter months due to the severe weather.

When we viewed the lake we all gasped, it was out of this world! It was absolutely beautiful, the reflections in the water at their best in the brilliant sunshine, chipmunks bobbing in and out between the rocks. Then we went to Lake Louise, known as the gem of the Rockies and very beautiful, but to us it didn't compare with Lake Moraine. Around the Lake were wooden boards commemorating the pioneers of the area. Lake Louise was discovered in 1882, eventually it was named Louise in honour of Queen Victoria's daughter. Passing where the Kicking Horse and Yoho Rivers meet, we started climbing, to negotiate the spiral bend by the Yoho River, the coach has to drive as near as possible to the precipice, then reverse up the hill, coming back down, the coach has to reverse downhill, a tricky procedure. We then went to the rail spiral tunnels in the Bow Water Valley, due to the steepness of the mountain, a way had to be found to negotiate the hill, otherwise the engine would be five metres lower than the carriages, so the train follows two loops through tunnels to lessen the steep, deep slope. It is strange to see the engine coming out of the tunnel and the carriages going into the tunnel

Moraine Lake with reflections from the sun

above! We then returned to Banff for another night, before continuing our journey, crossing the Continental divide at the North Saskatuan River and putting the clocks on one hour, then across the Icefields Parkway to the Columbia Icefield. After lunch we went by coach to the edge of the Icefield, where we transferred to the Sno-coach, which had enormous wheels. Each tyre costs 5,000 dollars, all specially built for glaciers. The maximum speed is 18 m.p.h. carrying 50 passengers, the journey is downhill then up a steep hill, once on the glacier, you get off the Sno-coach and walk on the glacier, before the return journey. Back on our coach our journey continued to the Athabasca Falls arriving at the Lobstick Lodge Hotel at Jasper. The next day, the intrepid ones of the party, including ourselves, took a short bus ride to the Athabasca River to go river rafting. We were given a plastic cape and lifejacket to wear and sign an accident waiver agreement. There were 15 in the boat including Rosa. The oarsman was in the centre of the boat. The sun shone as we glided down the river, we passed through eight rapids. To negotiate the rapids, the oarsman had to use all his strength as the boat turns around or sometimes remains broadside.

Walking on the glacier

It was an amazing, wonderful trip of one and a half hours, taking us down into Jasper, to be bussed back to the hotel. After a quick lunch, a coach arrived, which was picking up passengers from various hotels, the last one being the Jasper Park Hotel. The lakes nearby have Christian names, Mildred, Edith to name two. High on the mountains, were sheep and goats, on one of the lakes we saw two moose. Then we went to Malign Lake, which is quite high up and it had snowed during the night. We boarded a motorlaunch, two delightful young ladies were Captain and Courier. The boat sped across the lake towards Spirit Island, first meandering in the water for us to take in the views in brilliant sunshine, then we moored by the island for a short time to walk round a made trail, we talked to some artists, painting. Then back on the launch to return and board our coach, on the way back we saw three moose in a wooded area. In the grounds of Jasper

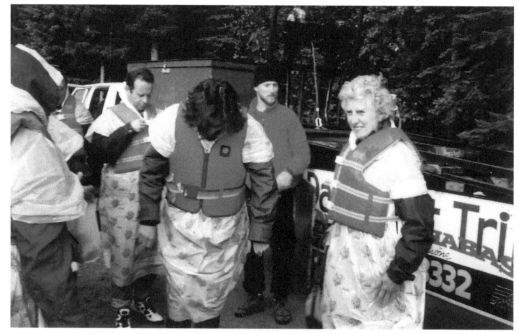
River rafting

Park we saw two male elks fighting for the female, they can be very dangerous at this time of the year. A photographer had to race to his car when one turned on him!

On our last evening, we walked through Jasper looking at the shops, which stay open late. As we neared the hotel, we were thrilled to clearly see the eclipse of the moon, also Saturn bright and clear.

We left Jasper after purchasing a sandwich lunch to eat on the coach. There was a watery sun, which developed into light rain. Our first stop was Mount Robson, the highest Canadian mountain, it is very rare to see the summit and the view can change within minutes. We continued our journey on the lookout for wildlife, then, on Highway 16, we saw a black bear, Isobel reversed back to give us a photocall, she thought it would be two to three years old. Shortly after this we stopped at a Trucker's café and washroom, then went on to Prince George. When we booked in at our hotel, we were officially welcomed. It was a lovely hotel in the centre of the town, we had a walk round, but it was drizzling, so we went back. We dined at the hotel and as we had a very early start the next morning, we went to bed early. We had

Totem Poles in Vancouver

been warned Friday and Saturday nights could be noisy, and it was! The Loggers made merry!

Wake up call was 5.00am, coffee was provided in the lobby and our bus came at 6.40am to take us to the BC Railway Station.

The British Columbia train left at 7.00am, the early part of the journey, it was misty and patchy, then the sun came out. The train track was narrow and twisting. The train only had two or three carriages initially, but more were added later. We had breakfast, lunch, afternoon tea and dinner on the train, all quite good and piping hot. There were some dramatic sights, but so far very little wildlife. Passenger trains had to give way to goods trains, which can be very long, causing delays.

We stopped at Allocet and were able to have a walk on the platform. The train followed the Fraser River on a single track, with occasionally a second rail, it was very narrow and winding, with the mighty Fraser far below. There

Foot of Grouse Mountain

were lovely lakeside views and on the intercom the driver said there was a grisly bear and two cubs up a tree, a little further down there were three black bears on the track. We passed through a lot of wooded areas, past lakes and waterfalls including the ski resort of Whistler and deep chasms. By this time it was dark and after dinner several of the party entertained us. Soon we saw the brilliant lights of Vancouver, marking the end of our long fascinating journey. Our coach took us to the Hotel Georgia, it was 10.00pm and we were ready for bed!

The next day, Sunday 29th September, after a continental breakfast, we boarded our coach for a City tour. Vancouver, like other cities, have many high rise blocks and more are planned, fortunately the 'City Fathers' have been persuaded to keep some heritage buildings. We went to Vancouver Park and Stanley Park, then on to Grouse Mountain, where we took the Gondola to the summit, unfortunately the mist did not lift soon enough to appreciate the views and nature trails. On the way down we spoke to some locals, who frequently jogged up the mountain and came down in the Gondola! Next, we went to the Capilano Suspension Bridge, which soars 230 feet above the Capilano River, stretching 450 feet across the Canyon. Since 1889, its spectacular beauty has attracted millions of visitors from all over the world. The first wire bridge replaced the hemp rope and wood bridge in 1903. The present bridge was built in 1956, when pre-stressed wire cables were encased in 13 tons of concrete at either end. The bridge sways somewhat and you receive a certificate to confirm your achievement if you walk both ways.

Muriel and a friend on the bridge

View point opposite the Capilano
Suspension Bridge

Apparently some people walk across one way, but cannot pluck up courage to walk back! We both made it both ways, receiving our certificates, but it was scary! The history of the area is interesting and the Park contains many carvings of Indians dating back to the 1930s. Lunch was in the hotel across the road from the bridge, during which we made a presentation to our courier Rosa, as some of the party were leaving. Our coach took us through an area called 'Gastown, then back to the hotel. In the late afternoon, we had a walk to buy food for tea and breakfast. There are many restaurants, but you have to search for food shops, eating out is the 'in thing'. Monday was the last full day of the organised tour, the coach came at 8.45am, picking up other tourists and drove to the ferry, 30 kilometres out of Vancouver, to go to Victoria. The ferryboat was enormous, transporting buses, lorries, cars and people. There was a restaurant on the 5th floor and the 6th deck was outside. The weather was warm and sunny, so we stayed on the top deck. The crossing took one and a half hours and it was enjoyable sailing between the Gulf Islands.

Victoria was more like England and our first stop in our coach was the Butchart Gardens, we had less than two hours to view the gardens, but were able to visit all the different areas of these beautiful grounds. There was a shop where you could buy seeds, cards and calendars. It was warm and we appreciated spoiling ourselves with a delicious strawberry yoghurt ice, before boarding the coach, to go to Victoria, passing expensive houses of the 'Uplands', there were large stone gates at either end of this district to determine the beginning and the end! We had one and a half hours to spend in Victoria, so we walked down to the harbour to the aquarium showing the sealife in the Pacific Ocean. There was a theatre, with an enormous tank, a scuba diver went in to the water to point out some of the fascinating specimens in the tank. He handled them so gently and carefully, one was an eel, but with a bigger body and tail, another was a giant octopus and many more. The coach then took us back to the ferry, where we were hoping to have a meal, but there was no vegetarian menu, all that was available was rice crispies and milk, and between us a small pot of yoghurt, slices of orange, one sandwich and one carrot bun! Back in Vancouver, the lights of the city were lovely, as we drove back to our hotel.

From the following day, we were on our own, travelling independently! Our bus to Seattle was due to leave at 12.30pm, so we had time to do our packing and walk to the shops to buy a sandwich, fruit and drinks for the journey. After many enquiries, we were told to go to Sandman, a hotel, for the bus, so we took a taxi to Sandman. We were a bit dubious, and asked again, to be told to go to Central Station which was15 minutes walk. Fortunately, we had left

Seattle from the train

ourselves with plenty of time! It was a lovely morning, so we decided to walk for the exercise! At last we were in the right place and boarded the bus at 12.15pm and we were given custom papers to complete, for when we arrived at the border in an hours time, then calamity! You are not able to take food or fruit into America,

Our cabins on the Amtrak train

anything you had would be confiscated!

To the amusement of the other passengers, within one hour, between us, we ate a large sandwich, two oranges, two apples and half a pound of grapes! At customs the bus had to be completely emptied and we had to take our suitcases and bags into the customs building. We were the only ones that had to pass through the International checkpoint, fill in yet another form and pay 12 US dollars for the privilege! We continued our journey arriving in Seattle at 3.30pm.

At this stage, our suitcases went through the baggage point and we didn't

Stretching our legs when the train stopped at a station

see them again until we arrived in Cleveland, Ohio, two and a half days and nights later! We were able to board the Amtrak train at 16.30pm, ready to leave at 16.50pm. The stewardess directed us to our cabin, on the a table was a half bottle of wine, two wine glasses, an aperitif food parcel, two picture cards of the train as a gift to us, also in the cabin, was a vase, with red roses and gypsophila, it was all superb and very comfortable. The train left on time, passing the harbour, sands, sea and hills in the background. There were lots of dogs on the sands, being exercised, the train ran at the side of the road, aptly named Railroad Avenue.

Instructions for meals were announced over the tannoy, then the restaurant waiter came round to give us a mealtime, we chose 5.30pm, the meal was excellent. We passed by Wallace Falls and State Park, the Falls were high up, then a tiny church, inviting travellers to pause for a prayer. There were steep rocks, with silver birch at the foot, interspersed with rivers and little hamlets, gradually, the sun set and it was dark.

The stewardess helped us organise the beds, they were very comfortable. The following morning after lovely hot showers, we had breakfast, all the meals are included in the fare when you book a sleeper. There was a beautiful sunrise over the mountains and lakes, but mist in the valley. We passed an Isaac Walton Hotel, a Glacier park and an Indian reservation with five teepee's. The land was rather barren, until we came to the American Prairies. In Manitoba there were enormous wheat stores, the railway is used to transport it. For lunch we had a salad and shared a slice of cheesecake and a fruit plate with cheese. Near Williston we saw oil wells with the pumps working, it was amazing how quickly the day passed, again we had a brilliant sunset.

On the last day of the Amtrac train journey, many were up early as some were leaving at St. Paul/Minneapolis. We were up early for breakfast, in order to be ready for a walk when the train stopped at 7.30am. The train left again at 8.20am, following the River Mississippi, it was frosty so there was a mist over the water, but it developed into a brilliant sunny day, passing beautiful scenery, parkland, camping sites and summer houses. The outskirts of

Chicago gave quite a bad impression, there was a lot of graffiti, but as we progressed to the centre, our impression improved, there was a water harbour with boats and the station was very modern. We had to change trains here and were assured our suitcases would be automatically transferred to the train for Cleveland. There was a large food emporium, but no vegetarian food! We boarded the train and we were in an ordinary carriage with lounger type seats which were very comfortable. The stewards checked the destination stations we all required and indicated above our seats the station, so we would be awakened in time to get off. We had a snack to tide us over and settled down for a nap! At 2.15am Friday 4th October, we arrived at Cleveland and the suitcases duly arrived in the baggage department. We took a taxi to the Omni International Hotel, a very luxurious hotel, which is connected to the Cleveland Clinic, one of the largest hospitals where they undertake open heart surgery. The room was superb, lovely, comfy beds, enormous easy chairs, television and refrigerator. We slept well, waking up at 9.00am, in time for breakfast.

We telephoned our cousin Joan, who would come to the hotel just before noon, which gave us time to have a look around. The vast lounge was beautifully furnished and all the revolving doors could accommodate wheelchairs, slowing them down to allow the wheelchair to pass through. Joan, with husband George, arrived in a massive car and after some photo calls, took us on a 'whistle stop' tour of Cleveland and Cleveland Heights, where her parents had lived. It was a lovely city and we went to the waterfront and had lunch on a floating restaurant. Whilst there we checked the greyhound bus timetables, then we went to their home at Cuyahoga Falls, via Brandywine Falls. Joan's house was a condominium, meaning they had a basement with a washroom, washer, dryer, shower and toilet. On the next floor, a dining room, lounge, kitchen and a bathroom, then upstairs three bedrooms and a bathroom, plus a double garage. Joan had invited all the family, from a wide area to come on the Saturday and Sunday to meet their English 'cousins' several times removed! Needless to say, the talking was non-stop. Joan had bought a lot of cookies and drinks. She also had an autograph book for all the relatives to write in, together with a photo, for us to be able to identify everyone. On the Sunday we went to church, two of the relatives had to leave after the sermon to get to the airport to fly home to Winsconsin. The rest of us went to a diner for a quick lunch, before our second 'at home' afternoon, followed by dinner in a lovely restaurant. It was completely a new experience for us to even have breakfast out!

The next day we visited those who, through age, had been unable to come at the weekend. Arrangements were made for cousin Walter and Evelyn to take us out to the Amish Country, Sugar Creek and Wilton area, the next day. We first visited a large shop, where you could buy in bulk, Walter always came for flour, and the marvellous selection of food, nuts and preserves. The Amish people made a lot of wooden items to sell in the shop, they also had an area for Christmas goods. Several of the shop assistants were wearing Amish dress. On the roads the Amish gigs were very much in evidence. We then went to a restaurant 'Alpine Alpha', built in Swiss style, with numerous cuckoo clocks. On the roof area is a house frontage, with a cuckoo clock, which strikes on the hour and figures come out and play instruments, for two dancers to dance to.

There is an Amish Visitor Centre, where you are taken around the old and new houses. The guide was a Mennonite, an older, but less strict order, she showed us how they live and dress, they do not have modern items such a television and a car, but they have a community telephone. This area has the largest number of Amish population, they seem to be very happy and joke a lot. Two girls, probably 17 or 18 years old, were in the kitchen baking bread, cookies and preserves.

We went for a ride in a gig and sat next to an Amish man, who passed the reins to us, but we thought the horses knew which way to go! There were barns for the animals and their farming is with horse drawn implements. The children, coming home from school, walk in single file. We went to a view point and we could see field upon field of sunflowers. You can tell an Amish

Amish Gigs

house from the washing on the line and no TV aerials. They have a three hour service on Sundays. It seems to be a very simple and well ordered life. We arrived back at 5.00pm after an enjoyable, interesting day.

We had two full days left, on one we went to the Quaker Centre in Akron, which had been taken over by the Hilton Hotel, the silos had been converted into bedrooms and there was quite a lot of interesting memorabilia, including in the restaurant, where we had lunch. In the afternoon, we visited another cousin, Brian, who lived in a bungalow, by a lake, he was not in the best of health. The day ended with an invitation for a meal with Erica and Paul 'Cordon bleu' cooks, so the meal was superb. We eventually rolled into bed at midnight!

On our last full day, we went to the 'falls' area, where a special clock had been refurbished by public subscription, the bricks on the wall surrounding it had the names of everyone who made a donation. We walked past the falls to the Sheraton Hotel, where we treated our lovely hosts to lunch. After a wander in the shops, we returned home to meet some of George's relatives, and enjoyed a relaxing evening with them all, then packed our cases, ready for a 5.30am alarm call, to set off for Cleveland at 6.40am!

PITTSBURGH
PENNSYLVANIA

The roads were busy, but we made good time, the bus was full, so we couldn't sit together, we set off at 8.30am with Joan and George waving goodbye! We arrived in Pittsburgh at 10.45am, where we had to change to the bus for New York, getting better seats. The driver was a delightful, coloured gentleman and he was very interesting to listen to. Although there are no real stops on the Greyhound buses he let us have several short stops and one half hour stop, when we went to a restaurant, but there was no vegetarian food. We eventually bought six breadcakes, 2 bananas, 2 yoghurts and a carton of milk, but nothing to put in the bread! A kindly manager heard our plight and gave us six thin slices of cheese! We went across the Pensylvania Highway, which had been built to negotiate a route through the Blue Mountain ridge. The driver told us this history! In 1850, the railroad had to go up an inclined plane by barge, the height was 1,270 feet, taking a Scotsman named Thompson, three days to travel between Philadelphia and Pittsburgh. Then three wealthy entrepreneurs, engaged five crews of engineers, to find the easiest way between the ocean and the lakes, and ten tunnels were built from 1850 to 1856, then it was all abandoned and it remained unused until 1937, when President Roosevelt with the clouds of war in Europe, said that America should be prepared by having an efficient transport system, so the Pennsylvania Highway was born. A single lane either way was opened in 1941 and there were seven tunnels, it was known as the Inner State Highway. The bridges were arch shaped to withstand 80 ton steam

Pennsylvania Turnpike

locos. The road was built with one foot of ballast, one foot of reinforced concrete and six inches of asphalt, to provide the first all weather highway in the world! Further developments were made in 1971 and in that year seven million cars went across the highway. The number of tunnels was reduced to four, with the length of the highway being 160 miles, tolls are paid. In 1996 nine to ten million vehicles crossed the highway.

We arrived in New York at 10.00pm, an Indian gentleman on the bus warned us not to engage in conversation with anyone who might approach us. So we went to the Left Luggage department, to leave the large suitcase and took a taxi to our hotel.

When we got to the hotel, they couldn't find the details of our booking, even though it had been paid in advance! They put all the problems down to celebrating Columbus weekend and they were so busy! They sorted out a room, which was basic, the beds were comfortable, the bathroom was built for thin people! But, at 11.00pm, we were happy to have a room and it was only for two nights.

There was no restaurant in the hotel, so we went out for breakfast, which was scrambled egg with an English muffin! It was a perfect day, with the sun shining, so we went to Pier 78, for a 90 minute river trip on the Hudson. It was sad to see the piers in poor repair, where once, the great liners such as

On the Hudson River

Pat in Central Park

the Queen Mary had docked. Some were being renovated, one was an indoor tennis court, another was made into a car pound. The guide pointed out the various areas and buildings, Manhattan, Brooklyn Bridge, United Nations, Universities, the largest free standing clock and we went quite close to the Statue of Liberty and Ellis Island. In the afternoon, we walked up Broadway and booked two seats for the evening show at the Ethel Barrymore Theatre. Then we went to Central Park, it was amazing to see such a lovely park in the middle of a chaotic city! There were many entertainers, a band, a clown, a juggler, a flautist, fireeater, and keyboard players, also many talented artists. The road around the perimeter was a haven for walkers, joggers, roller skaters, skate borders and cyclists. There was a children's zoo and a mechanical clock on an archway, after the clock chimed, animals parade around to the music of 'Frere Jacques'. On 34th Street, we went inside the Empire State Building,

It was only a peep to this palatial building, as there were long queues. We had tea in our room, then took a taxi to the theatre to see Oscar Wilde's 'An Ideal Husband', most of the cast being English – Anna Cateret, Michael Denison and Dulcie Gray, so we really enjoyed the show. We managed to hail a taxi to get back to the hotel, as the streets were chaotic, with horns blasting.

In the morning, we walked to the bus station, collected the large case and made our way to Gate 78, for the bus to Montreal.

Central Park mechanical clock. Animals move around to 'Frere Jacques'

The countryside was spectacular, passing Mohawk River, Barge Canal, Hamilton, Saratoga Country National Park and Spa Town, the Adirondack Mountain, Glen Falls, Lake George, Schoon Lake, a glimpse of Lake Placid, the Keene Valley, arriving at Montreal at 7.00pm. Again, we left our large case in a locker and took a taxi to Le Meridien Hotel, we had a lovely room for the night. It was Thanksgiving weekend, so facilities were limited.

The next day, after breakfast in the mall, we walked to the bus station for the 10.00am bus to Quebec. We boarded a 'bendy bus' for the journey, which was quite comfortable, the countryside was flat and mainly arable, arriving in Quebec at 1.00pm. We bought a map, then walked up the hill, to the Radisson Hotel, where we were booked in for three nights. It was a lovely hotel, unfortunately, there was a strike on and strikers were parading outside with placards, but they didn't bother us, the hotel gave us a complimentary continental breakfast each day. Our room was number 1086, overlooking the St. Lawrence Waterway, on looking at the visitor's guide, to our delight, found a Vegetarian Restaurant, quite close to the hotel.

It was well designed for both hot and cold meals, we were both given a large glass plate and helped yourself to whatever and as much as we wanted, your plate was weighed and you paid accordingly. For later on, we bought sandwiches, date squares, fruit, fruit juice and water, depositing them in our hotel room and went for a walk around the city wall, and the shops. We had promised a friend in Castleton, to visit Gill, who lived in Quebec, so we rang and arranged to visit her the following evening. In order to see as much as possible, the next morning, we booked to go on two tours at the reception, before going on a short walk, the sun was brilliant, but it was cold and windy, needing woollies and ear protectors! A bus picked us up at 10.00am, taking us to Frontenac Square to join the tour bus, which took us to the Parliament building, Duffen Promenade, the Plains of Abraham, the Citadel, then to the dock area, returning to Chateau Frontenac at 12 noon.

Our afternoon tour started at 1.00pm, so we had just 55 minutes to find lunch, an obliging restaurant provided us with celery soup and rolls, followed by cheese omelette and vegetables, just in time for our second tour!

Our first stop was to the Montmorency Falls and Park where a cable car takes you to the summit of the Falls or you can go by bus, Muriel went by bus, Pat by cable car! The sun was shining, which created a rainbow at the foot of the Falls. The bus then took us across the bridge, over the St Lawrence, to the Ile d'Orean, a delightful, peaceful area, with very nice houses. The residents were adamant that they did not want the Island changing, refusing a shopping complex, neither was there any wildlife. Back on the mainland, we went towards St. Anne, then the driver diverted down a road to call at Chez Marie, who bakes her own bread and for two dollars (£1), you get a cup of coffee and a slice of bread spread with Maple Butter. We saw several storage houses built into the rock on the roadside, they are used for storing apples and other goods. Then we went to a Bee-Keeping establishment, where they made mead and other honey products, we were able to walk around the small factory and watch the bees, the queen bee had been marked and was larger that the

Muriel with Gill in her flat

working bees. It takes at least nine months to make mead. The last visit was to St Ann's Basilica, an enormous, ornate, Roman Catholic church, there was a service in progress and though visitors were walking around, we felt it was an intrusion, so had a walk outside. We arrived back at the Radison at 5.00pm. After buying sandwiches, we walked to meet Gill, which took us about 30 minutes, she lived in a very pleasant flat near the Plains of Abraham, she and her beautiful black cat, gave us a lovely welcome and in spite of saying we would take a sandwich with us, she had prepared a lovely meal. We took some pictures and talked non-stop until after 10.00pm, then walked back to the hotel.

Wednesday 16th October was our last full day in Quebec, a cloudy but fine day. We walked to the bus station to check the bus times, then on to the Harbour front where a Farmer's market was in progress, selling bags and bags of apples, crab apples, vegetables, potatoes, pumpkins and plums. The markets continue to the end of October. We went to the ferry, taking a return trip across the St. Lawrence, to the south bank, enjoying good views of Quebec and passing boats. On returning, we walked up the Artists Road, buying some pictures, by Indian artists.

We had lunch at Le Commensal Vegetarian restaurant, buying our tea at the same time, taking it back to the hotel, before returning to Frontenac, walking around Petite Champlain, a busy thoroughfare, along Dufferin Promenade.

Farmers Market in Quebec

Then climbing the 310 steps to the Plains of Abraham, past the Citadel, taking a different way back to the hotel.

The bus back to Montreal left at 11.00am, so after breakfast, we took a walk beyond the hotel, to Rue Levesque Boulevard. The gardeners were preparing for the winter, by wrapping the trees with fleece and twine and erecting plastic shields. Then turning down to reach Rue St Jean, where we knew we could buy something for lunch, to eat on the bus. Returning to collect our luggage and catch the bus.

We arrived at 2.00pm in Montreal, we collected our big suitcase, then filled a locker with most of our luggage, so we could have a last walk in Montreal to Fontaine Park, returning to the bus station to collect the luggage and catch the 3.50pm Airport bus, arriving at Mirabel Airport at 5.00pm.

We went through the initial check to get rid of the luggage, leaving us time to have a drink and watch the beautiful red sunset. The plane left on time at 7.30pm, dinner was served at 9.00pm. We then catnapped. During the night, the watches were advanced six hours, so around 5.15am we were served a light snack and from our window seats, we were able to watch the lights below, as we flew up the Severn Estuary and on to London, the River Thames and bridges clearly visible, landing at Heathrow at 6.45am.

After getting through customs quickly, the hardest part was finding the bus to take us to London, it was 8.20am before we boarded the bus, which only went to Euston, so we had to walk to St Pancras.

The train to Sheffield was at the platform and we boarded the First Class compartment, then had an enormous breakfast, arriving in Sheffield at 1.30pm. The Hope Valley train left at 3.15pm, arriving at Hope Station at 3.45pm, with a smiling Gerald, our neighbour, to meet us.

Needless to say, we had a busy time on arriving home, just a week later, we hosted the Church of England Flower Arrangers Workshop in the Village Hall, catering for 36! Then we started our four year course 'Education for Ministry', it originated from the University of the South, Tenessee. It was interesting, but time consuming!

Each year, we had to spend 36 sessions, of three hours, with our group of seven, including our mentor, also three to four hours each week of private study and preparation.

On top of this, we had to get the 'wheels in motion' for the Senior Citizens Christmas lunch on December 14th, catering for 80-100. Somebody has to start getting the numbers and the cooks, the villagers are very generous and we get lots of help. In November, Muriel had to go to Newcastle for a meeting and we stayed a night with friends nearby. By chance there was a Canine Defence League Kennel nearby, so we called in. Of course, who could resist a three-month old black and tan bitch, that had been abandoned in an empty house? So we adopted Wendy, we had quite a long journey, but she behaved perfectly and we rang the kennels when we arrived home as requested. It was great to have a dog again.

Our new arrival, Wendy!

Cassie. Then there were two!

About three months later, we felt it would be good for Wendy to have a mate, so we all went to the Leeds Canine Defence League. There was a little dog called Cassie, who had been found as a young puppy wandering in Leeds, she was taken to the kennels and adopted by a man, but he couldn't manage her and took her back to the kennels. For the next two to three months, everyone passed her by. We liked her, but when we put Wendy in, she dominated Cassie. Then the kennel lady suggested that she put her Jack Russell in with Wendy and she immediately cowered. So we all felt, with patience, this could be overcome, so we signed the adoption papers. Before we could take her, the kennels vet had to check her over. Pat thought the vet was a bit rough, looking down her throat, but we were able to take her. All the way home Cassie was travel sick, she was such a mixed up puppy, but with patience and kindness, she was soon house trained and short trips in the car, got her used to it and the travel sickness gradually abated.

Horseplay!

The dogs were of a similar age and got on well together, we called them 'double trouble', they would egg each other on and have a lot of horseplay. They loved long walks and it helped to keep us fit!

We were both in the Village Pantomime which was Peter Pan, Pat was Tinkerbell! She only appeared in her fairy finery at the end, when she pronounced the epilogue, in the earlier parts, the fairy was portrayed by a special light flitting around the stage, it was very effective. Both of us performed in a line dance as lost boys. Muriel was also a 'lost boy' in the final scene. It was a lot of fun.

We again opened our garden for the two Organic Gardening weekends in June and August. Preparing the garden was a nightmare, with two puppies causing mayhem! One lawn was known as the 'puppies lawn' due to all the yellow patches. We raised £758.00 for the High Peak Hospice and £80.00 to the Organic Research Association.

We had a few holidays in the trailer tent, Weston- Super Mare, Criccieth, Barnard Castle, Leek, Kingsbury, Kirby Bain and five days in a bungalow, near Filey, to coincide with a hand bell ringing rally in Scarborough.

In 1998 we had a lot of rain, fortunately we didn't have flooding. Muriel despaired, trying to get the garden shipshape, for the two Organic weekends.

Our project that year was to raise money for a Loop and Enhanced Sound System in church. The cost was £3,000.00, a local charitable club, gave a donation of £900. In March, we started selling marmalade, lemon curd, chutneys and cakes, so with the money raised by the two weekends, we had reached our goal, and the system was soon installed.

A new Vicar was also installed, he had three parishes to cover, Bradwell, Hope and Castleton. They lived in the Bradwell Vicarage, which was the obvious choice. He was a little older, which was probably best, to sort out the changes and he had lots of common sense.

We had two holidays in our trailer tent, the first in May, when we went to Tarland, between Aberdeen and Ballater, quite a long journey, so we stayed one night in a hotel at Kirkholm on the way up and at Lauderdale on the way down. The campsite was adjacent to an enormous wood, with rabbits abound! The dogs were in their element.

In September, we went to Sandringham, for a much needed break, between the two Horticultural Society Shows. The start of 1999 was rain and more rain! Eventually we were ready for the two Organic Gardening weekends, this year we made a 'slug proof' vegetable patch, four feet square, it is surrounded by a moat made out of guttering, it was very successful (and still is), the visitors were interested and Muriel hoped to have lettuce free of slug damage! The two weekends raised £1,070.00 for local charities.

The pantomime that year was 'Treasure Island', Pat was Bertha Gunn, a rather scruffy, potty, ex-pirate, who had been marooned on the island for three years, it was great fun.

It was our third year in the Education for Ministry course, which we both enjoyed, although it was hard work, with a lot of reading. For the annual workshop at West Hill College near Birmingham, the speaker was David Jenkins, the ex-Bishop of Durham. He was an amazing person, who gave us much 'food for thought'.

We had a steady flow of engagements throughout the year, for hand bell

Fun on the sands with Pat

ringing, as well as going round the pubs and restaurants at Christmas, raising an appreciable amount of money for charities

We cannot say we looked forward to all the 'razzmatazz' accompanying the Millennium events. On New Year's Eve, we would be in the lounge with the dogs, the television on loud to hide the noise of fireworks. Cassie was very frightened, panting and shivering, which made Wendy bark! They had a

Time to go home.
From our favourite Sandringham site

homeopathic remedy, which helped a little. We were prepared to toast the New Year in, with a glass and mince pies at the ready!

Part VI

Village Life

January 1st 2000, was a beautiful, sunny day, it had been pre-arranged that those interested would climb to the summit of Mam Tor to see the sunrise!

There was a steady trek of villagers walking, some like us, with our two dogs, went by car to the foot of the mountain, then climbed to the summit. Those of us who arrived early, were rewarded, by seeing a perfect sunrise. Altogether, around 250 eventually arrived on the mountain, many brought their breakfasts and drinks and there was a happy, holiday atmosphere, which we all enjoyed.

Ringing in the Millennium

At 12 noon, it had been suggested, that all the Church Tower bells in the country should ring out at that time, to welcome in the Millennium. St. Edmund's eight tower bell ringers, including both of us, joined in and rang the church bells for 30 minutes. The landlord at the George and his wife, brought us coffee, rum and Christmas cake, on completion of the ring.

The addition to the family. Emma on the left and Iffy

The next day, a Village Treasure Hunt was organised, which took us to every part of the village, most of us eventually solved all the clues!

On the 3rd of January, we had an S.O.S. from friends in Lincolnshire, asking us to fetch their dogs, as they could no longer cope with them. We hastily made sandwiches, packed the dogs' lunches and set off. Apparently, Dick had a fall just after Christmas and developed pneumonia, he went into hospital and died a fortnight later. His wife, Alison, wanted us to keep the dogs, as we had promised we would. The dogs were Emma, a cross bearded collie/afghan, 13 years old and Iffy a cross collie/retriever nine years old. Our dogs were very good, allowing them in the car, they seemed to understand something was wrong, so, with the car piled high with dog beds, collars, leads and dog food, we were on the way home.

Our lives had changed overnight, with four bitches, it was a learning curve! To cut a long story short, once we got the pecking order sorted out, with Emma the oldest, who thought she should be the top dog! Our arms grew 12 inches longer and our legs 12 inches shorter with all the walks, on most days it was two walks of about an hour each time! Feeding times could create problems, keeping

A day out at Fountains Abbey

We are giving us a bit of space!

Who will win?

them apart, so that they all got a fair share.

In February, we went to stay in a farm cottage at Belford, in Northumberland and the four dogs were welcome. It was a lovely part of the country, with the sand, sea and long country walks. We stayed for almost a week and had a super time, with probably more sunshine than in the summer. In July, we went to South West Wales in the trailer tent, having almost two weeks of relatively good weather, apart from a force eight gale. This made us realise that we should have a 'tie down' for the trailer, so we went into Haverford West to buy one, which we have used since on many occasions. Whilst there, we called at a dog shop and we were introduced to Burns dog food, which the dogs loved.

When we arrived home, we tried to purchase it at our dog shop in Bakewell. They hadn't heard of it, but eventually tracked the makers down, to be told they were only a small family firm, but they would send some. It is strange how from then on it has become our pet shop's most popular dog food!

In September, we went to Sandringham for ten days, the weather was mixed, including a vicious thunderstorm in the middle of the night, two of the dogs were petrified and landed on top of us shivering. The weather then improved a little and we enjoyed the break.

The line up!

During the year, we opened the garden for two National Organic Gardening Weekends, with surprisingly good weather and we had an excellent response, sending £200.00 to the Henry Doubleday Research Unit, £300.00 to the local Hospice Day Care Centre and £458.00 to the Village School.

In July, we commenced our fourth year of the Education for Ministry course. All being well, we Graduate in July next year. We found it a very interesting course, but history does repeat itself!

We had several hand bell ringing engagements and we started teaching some of the village schoolchildren to ring. Our ringing over the Christmas period enabled us to send £500.00 to Save the Children Fund.

Our first major event in 2001 was a Flower Festival, May 5th to the 13th, it seemed very relevant that we should depict Christ's life and "In his Steps" was an appropriate title. Our aims were to provide an event which would give our visitors "food for thought" together with an understanding of our Lord's life, through flowers and a spiritual experience. We were fortunate to be able to call on expert flower arrangers, to undertake the interpretation in flowers. There were 14 flower arrangements from the Birth of Christ to the Passover and a local friend, Margaret Hickinson, an expert in calligraphy, wrote each card, with the title of the arrangement.On the Sunday afternoon, we had a Songs of Praise, with members of the congregation introducing the hymns on the theme of the festival. The Hope Valley College "Big Band"

Hand bell ringing in church for Save the Children

gave a memorable, talented performance to a large audience.

During this time there was a Foot and Mouth scare, but in spite of this, the ten days of the festival was a resounding success, raising £3,687.14 for St. Edmund's Church.

Our next thrill was in July, when we went to Westhill College, Birmingham, to receive our

'In his Steps' The Baptism of Jesus

Diplomas, for the four year course of 'Education for Ministry' which we had completed in June. We had a great day and we were so thrilled that our Vicar, Peter Bowles, was able to be there for this momentous occasion.

Education for Ministry Diplomas after four years studying

With all the excitement, we didn't have a chance to get away in the trailer tent until September, when we had 11 nights in Sandringham and six in Woodhall Spa. We had a super holiday, the dogs had a marvellous time, with lots of walks. Whilst we were away, we went to three dog shows, Emma at over 14 years old, won a large cup, two small trophies and seven rosettes, the other three managed one rosette each, albeit that Cassie's was really a booby prize!'

During the summer months we had a Gardeners' Club, for six village schoolchildren, once a week. They did a variety of tasks, e.g. sowing seeds, taking cuttings, transplanting. We had to stop for the winter months but started again in the spring. We also had eight children once a week for hand bell ringing. Again our Christmas hand bell ringing raised £500.00 for Save the Children Fund.

To end the year, we decided that four dogs, plus the two of us, in a two door, Peugeot 206 hatchback, was not the safest mode of transport, so we bought a Peugeot Partner Combi, with an enormous boot, four doors, two of which were sliding. This gave us much more space.

Weekly hand bell practice with children

2002.

Our year started in fine style in January, by going on holiday! A cottage had been booked at Crackington Haven, Cornwall, for a week. On the way down, we stayed two nights in a hotel in Axbridge, near Cheddar and on the way back, two nights at Belford in the Cotswolds, having four dogs was not a problem. The holiday was

Who's for a paddle?

good, apart from one rainy day and we were able to visit the Lost Gardens of Heligan, the Eden Project, and visit a friend in St Trevene, near Helston. The new car, which we call the 'dogmobile', was super for the six of us, with more space for the luggage and dog's bean bags. The cottage was excellent and there was a huge field leading to a coastal path.

In July, Emma, over 15 years had a 'doggy stroke', she responded well to a vasodilator and a homeopathic tablet daily. She wasn't able to walk as far as the other three, but was upset if she was left behind, the solution was a pram! At a local car boot sale, we bought a Brittax pram for £5.00 – a 'Callis' conversion and hey presto, a very comfy seat on the parcel tray. She looked like a queen sitting there, taking everything in. Several people asked if they could take her picture, including the Animal Behavourist, Dr. Roger Mudford, whom we met at a dog show in the September.

Wendy and Cassie, both now six years old, went to agility classes, Pat would be two hours charging round, over jumps, an 'A frame', tunnels, seesaw, a walkway, weaving sticks and onto a table. Cassie, the rascal, was pure entertainment value! Iffy at 12 years old, liked nothing better than playing with a ball or some other play toy.

Our second long holiday in the trailer tent was again in Sandringham and Woodhall Spa, we went in that area so that we could take the dogs to see Alison, who was then in a care home, in Woodhall Spa.

During the summer, June and August, we had two Organic Gardening weekends, raising £904.00, dividing it between Organic research, the village school, the Canine Defence League and the World Society for the Protection of Animals.

We continued to produce for the W.I. Market, we also tried to cut down, not very successfully, due to covering for others. The Gardeners Club and hand bell ringing, from the village school, continued to make progress. The ringers had two or three short performances. We were able to raise £500.00 for Save the Children Fund again.

Having enjoyed the January holiday in 2002 so much, we booked a holiday, starting January 4th in 2003 and we were blessed with good weather again! The accommodation was a delightful wooden chalet near

Alison was pleased to see the dogs

The chalet near Minehead

The walk into Minehead

Minehead. The owners lived in a large house in the extensive grounds. There were six chalets and two more were in the process of being erected, but at that time, we were the only occupants.

We were able to walk into Minehead, through pleasant parkland and enjoyed exploring the area in such good weather, the week passed all too quickly. Carrying on with the holiday theme, we had ten days in our favourite haunts, Woodhall Spa and Sandringham in the trailer tent.

In June and August, we advertised our Organic Gardening weekends as usual and we had a telephone call from the Derbyshire Times, asking if they could come and see us for an article in the newspaper. They asked lots of questions and took photographs, the headlines on the 5th June was 'Organic Pairs'

Copyright Sheffield Telegraph

garden secrets'. This was followed by the Sheffield Telegraph, wanting to interview us and their article was published on June 13th, with the heading 'I'm a crustacean, get me out of here'. So with all this excellent press coverage, we were extra busy and the four weekends raised £1,250.00 which was divided between the various charities.

In August the 'shows' kept us busy. Muriel as Secretary of the Horticultural section at the Hope Show, while Pat was asked to judge the Cookery section at two shows and the Preserves at the Hope Show, as well as helping Muriel! It was customary to auction items from the entries that had been left, the usual auctioneer was unable to continue, so Pat took on the role for a few years, until we found an excellent replacement in Castleton's Chris Gill.

During our previous holiday, we decided that the trailer tent was getting a bit heavy for us, particularly the awning, which was made of PVC and lifting it onto the poles was proving a problem, so we decided to sell it and look for a small caravan. During the holiday, we had met a club member, who owned an Eriba Puck and they were pleased to show us around. It seemed ideal for us, so we contacted the firm and placed an order for one.

At the end of July 2003, we went to collect our Eriba Puck, staying overnight at a nearby camping club site. It was a small two berth, so with four dogs we were like sardines in a tin! The awning gave us quite a bit more space. Considering the size, it is very well constructed, with a pop up roof, giving height, an electric refrigerator, a gas grill, a wardrobe and an appreciable amount of storage space, the 'icing on

Emma with the cups and rosettes she won.
With Iffy, Wendy and Cassie

the cake' was that it could be stored at home in the garage!

So, in September, we had three weeks holiday, eight nights at Kessingland in Suffolk, seven nights in Sandringham and five nights in Wooodhall Spa. The weather was brilliant, in fact it was so hot, we were very lazy! Our final jaunt was in October, when we had three nights in the Lake District near Windermere, with super weather. The dogs were fine, Emma over 16, was a 'downhill' walker, getting pushed up the hills in the pram. Iffy at 13 was very active and always hungry! Wendy had to stop going to agility, she became lame, which improved with homeopathy. She was more heavily built than Cassie, who revelled in agility, with Pat dashing round with her!

Unfortunately, 2004 started with sadness, when 17 year old Emma, died at the end of February. She was a lovely dog. When we took her to the dog shows, she won all the classes she entered. She accepted using the pram following her stroke, to continue regular walks. We all missed her very much, but she'd had a long, loving, good life.

We had decided to undertake our third Flower Festival, we had already started to do some preparatory work the previous year. The theme was 'Love Conquers All' and we soon realized the enormity of the title and all the hard work we had to do, before the opening, on the 1st of May.

The Festival was a resounding success. For the first time, we decided to have a preview night, for those who had helped in any way, also those who would be stewarding, so we could explain the complex 14 arrangements. St. Valentine was depicted as legend states in prison, to assure all his friends of his friendship and love, he reached out, picked a bunch of violets and the dove took them to his followers with the message 'I love you'. On another window, there was a large spider's web and attached to it were all the things that love rejects, for the spider to crush them. On the opposite wall was a rainbow, with the meanings of the word 'Love' ending with a 'crock of gold, signifying 'God's Promise' to the world. The 13th arrangement was called 'Peace and tranquillity', with white lilies, greenery and interspersed by pieces of Blue John stone, which is thought to have healing properties, wellbeing, as well endorsing the title.

Events like this, with so many helping, unite a village and there were many, nice, comments written in the visitors book. It was also a fitting event for our Vicar, who had worked so hard, uniting the three villages and later in the year was due to retire. The festival raised £2,120.00 for church funds.

Now down to three!

To recharge the batteries, we went to Woodhall Spa, to let Alison see Iffy and tell her Emma had died. Back home we prepared for the Organic Gardening weekends, being fortunate having good weather, raising over £1,000.00.

At the end of July, the Cross Breed and Mongrel Club, of which we are members, organised a rally at Bassenthwaite, in the Lake District, the dogs had a grand time on the sands, it was good to share four nights with the club.

Our main holiday was in September, going east for the better weather, returning to Kessingland, a good centre, just six miles north of Southwold, a delightful area. A dental nurse friend, Geraldine lived in the village of Pulham St. Mary, not too far away, so we called to see her. In conversation, she told us about the Christmas Tree Festival held in their church, showing us pictures. It was due to this visit, that we decided in 2008 to have a Christmas Tree Festival in St Edmund's Church.

On the way home we had four nights at St. Neots, to go to a Dog Show. The previous year, Emma had won a trophy which we had to return. Cassie now eight, came fifth in the fastest recall, out of about 100 entries.

Locally, at the end of our lane, they were building five houses by the river, the weather was poor and it became a quagmire, to add to this, the outdoor centre up the lane, were enlarging their pond, into what looked like a lake, so there was mud and more mud, not good for dog walks!

We raised £780.00 hand bell ringing over the Christmas period, which was donated to Village Ventures (Africa), based in Bakewell, they send volunteers to help the people in areas with many small villages to become self sufficient.

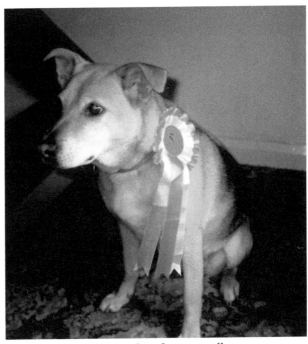

Cassie 5th in fastest recall

At the start of 2005 there was the Tsunami Disaster, in the Indian Ocean. Something had to be done quickly! If someone gives a push, our village is most generous. So we set the 'wheels in motion' and the village responded and we still have the receipts from the Post Office showing that in just over three weeks 'Six and a Half Thousand' was raised, much of which being 'gift aided'. This was raised by an enormous Coffee Morning in the village hall, two auctions, collecting tins in all the shops, restaurants and pubs and generous donations. We continued having weekly stalls in Church during January, when the appeal closed.

We had almost forgotten that we had booked the decorator weeks ago, he arrived on January 10th, to decorate downstairs, followed by the carpet cleaner! So in April, we decided a three week holiday was due! We packed the caravan and made for Scotland. The first night we stayed at Luss, on the banks of Loch Lomond, then we went to Inverewe in the North West for eight nights. The scenery was superb, although we had gales for two days up to 80 mph. We then went on the East coast to the Black Isle, staying at Rose Markie, camping by the sea shore. From there we went to Scone, Perthshire, ending up at Windermere for the last three nights. Apart from the two days of gales, we had good weather.

On the Banks of Loch Lomond

In May, the new Vicar was installed, who was looking forward to living in the Hope Valley! We opened the garden in June for one weekend, it was a good job we didn't open in August, by then the garden was well past its best.

Iffy was getting old so when we went to Sandringham we took the pram. These gardens were near by

There had been an enormous amount of growth, with everything being a month early! We rounded the camping season off with ten nights in Sandringham, four nights in St Neots and in October four nights at Ravenglass, before putting the caravan away for the winter.

So far we had been blessed with good health, apart from the 'knees playing up'. Pat has glaucoma, which now necessitates one drop in each eye at bedtime, to keep the pressures behind the eyes within a normal level. I go

The Frienship Club remembering V.E. day with a 'street party', Pat stood on the left. Muriel stood on the right

every six months, privately, to see the Opthamologist. This was because at the Hallamshire Hospital, I saw a different person at each visit, then they lost my notes! Now I see the same doctor each time and car parking is available.

Looking for a bargain

We have previously mentioned the Friendship Club, which continued to flourish, for a number of years. We were very fortunate for the outings to have Sheila as Chairman of the club and a

It was such a hot day - the bus overheated!

driver for the Community bus. In the earlier days, our members filled the bus and Pat took the overflow in her car! Sometimes it would be for a full day and other times, a half day's outing. Over the years, high on the list of popular visits, was Garden centres, where you could always get a drink, light refreshments or a meal. We have probably been in every centre between Ashbourne, Chatsworth and Sheffield. We visited numerous well dressings, Litton was always popular, with the children Maypole dancing. A special treat was a trip and meal on the Canal boat. In the winter evenings we supported Bradwell and Hathersage Pantomines as well as our local ones. Occasionally, we would have a speaker, one spoke about her day at Derby Cathedral, when the Queen was presenting the 'Maundy Money'. The members were more than happy to play Whist, Scrabble, Dominoes, jig saw puzzles, in the village hall, with a cup of tea/coffee, biscuits and a chat.

Every year the members supported the Samaritan Purse appeal, when you filled a shoe box with gifts for Children at Christmas time. In the early days of the club, we would have over 30 boxes, they had to be in by the beginning of November. Usually on New Year's Eve, we would have a lunchtime meeting, with homemade soup, bridge rolls, tea, coffee and cake, followed with a game of bingo, with prizes for winners. For the energetic, finishing with the 'hokey cokey' and everyone joining in, either standing or seated, with 'Auld Lang Syne'.

Muriel and pat, second and third from the left, ringing at Hathersage Church

Gradually, the numbers deteriorated, due to ill health and age. The newcomers to the village rarely joined in. Eventually we only had five or six members, in the large village hall, we could not afford the hire charge, so it was mutually decided in 2015 to 'call it a day'.

A similar occurrence unfortunately happened with the hand bell ringing. When we first started ringing in Castleton, a group from Hathersage contacted us. They were short of ringers, they had a larger set of hand bells,

Pat, Muriel and Kath at the Castle Pub

so the two of us went to join them for practice every Monday. It was good to ring with a larger group and we did concerts in their church. Some of the members were a little older than us and again, ill health and age, took its toll. It was sad, that in both villages, the general public loved to hear the hand bells, but it was very hard to get ringers!

It was amazing that three of us in Castleton, Kath, Muriel and Pat, playing four bells each, were able to play such a range of music. To play four in hand, is easier on the lighter bells, Kath played the four slightly heavier bells off the table as you will see in one of the photographs. Our bells were in tune with each other, but not in tune with the larger sets of bells. When we went to rallies, we always had a selection of music ready for when it was our turn to perform and it was always well received. The three of us were proud that our ringing raised hundreds of pounds for various charities and also provided entertainment on so many occasions, whether it was in church, the church yard, old people's homes, clubs, restaurants and pubs. Sadly, Kath became ill and died in August 2006. We missed her very much as a neighbour, a very good friend, who was always ready to join in and 'have a go', whether it was while holidaying with us on the canals, helping with all our events, looking after a stall in the garden or house, or sharing her expertise with bell ringing, we enjoyed lots of fun and laughter.

There were several engagements booked and we were grateful to two neighbours, Val and Lindsay, who helped out on a few occasions, when they had no work commitments. We were able to ring some of the easier carols using eight bells, carrying on until 2007. We also continued with the schoolchildren. We took them several times to play at Moorland Care Home in Hathersage. This continued, until the children had to start practicing only during their dinner break, when they wanted play. So what with that and Muriel suffering with Macular degeneration, the hand bells were put into storage!

As members of the Church of England Flower Arrangers Association (CEFAA), Pat was currently the Chairman of the Derby Branch, we were keen to have a Flower Festival on the theme 'Derbyshire Life'. We began the preparation in 2006, to be ready for it to take place the following year, May 26th to June 3rd. They wanted St. Edmund's Church to host it, as we attracted the most visitors in North Derbyshire. It was a big task, with over 24 areas of life to bring in. We started by the members deciding which aspect they would like to undertake and the preparations got underway! In the end, 2007 turned out to be a year you never forget!

After ten years of editing the Parish Magazine, Ray Fowler wished to resign, but no one came forward to take over and it seemed that the magazine would finish! In a weak moment, Pat said this must not happen, although she knew nothing about editing and knew that Ray would be a hard act to follow, said she would have a go! So on January 1st our first magazine was published! I was very grateful to Steve Hays (a computer wizard), for his help and guidance, always ready to get me out of trouble. Before we got our 'act together' we were grateful to Jon and Emma, who printed our earlier editions. In the end, we purchased a new printer, which was much quicker, printing the increasing numbers of magazines.

There were eight, monthly, magazines to publish in the year, the other four months, a village publication 'Peveril Post is distributed in the village.

Iffy always liked to lick out.
She was a lovely dog

Adverts for local businesses were important to help fund the magazine. We needed and got more, by the end of March, our deadline. Steve then prepared them for printing, by a local firm, producing enough for the year. As soon as we started using the adverts in the June magazine, we were able to send the accounts to the advertisers, the magazine then became self-supporting. A local artist, Sonya Sprinthall, donated a pen and ink drawing of the church for the outside cover, which was greatly admired.

I enjoyed editing the magazine, although at times it could be frustrating! Muriel helped with proof reading and the stapling. It was like a conveyer belt and a relief when the 280 magazines were ready for our excellent team of distributers.

Sadly on March 16th, Iffy the cross border Collie, died aged 16 years 5 months, she had been going downhill for a few months, but we took her out in the pram, that we had used for Emma. This was followed by Wendy not being well, she played with her food and was reluctant to walk far. We took her to the vet and blood tests showed she had severe renal failure, a ghastly problem with no known cure. We decided we would have a short break in the

It was terrible when Wendy died so young

Cassie was a lost soul, but we gave her
lots of love

caravan in April, to her favourite place, Woodhall Spa and she enjoyed walking in Ostler woods. When we returned home, she soon started to deteriorate and on May 7th we had to make the horrible decision, she was ten years 8 months old.

We were all devastated and little Cassie, who had never been on her own, couldn't understand what was happening, she didn't like being left alone, but we gave her lots of love.

In the midst of all this, we had a Christian Aid Collection to organise, the Flower Festival on Derbyshire Life, and the Open Garden weekend in the middle of June! As if this was not sufficient, Muriel had been losing weight for some months, with Pat nagging her to see the GP, but she insisted she was alright.

Pat thought Muriel had a thyroid problem and when her weight was down to seven stone, she was finally persuaded to see the GP! Her blood test showed she had hyperthyroidism and was immediately put on tablets, but our GP wanted her to see an Endocrinologist, as the level in her serum blood was 36! (normal is 3 to 6). To get an early appointment, we went privately and were seen the day before the flower festival opened.

Her delay in going to the GP, had affected her heart, with an irregular pulse rate, up to around 150! To cut a long story short, during the next few weeks she had many tests, numerous drugs and eventually her heart rhythm

At the opening of the festival 'Derbyshire Life'

The White Lady in Devon

was normal and, after a while, she was able to reduce some of the tablets.

On a brighter note, the Flower Festival featuring 'Derbyshire Life', was a great success. It was opened by our previous Vicar, Rev. Peter Bowles and his wife Alison, who came over from Norfolk for the occasion. There was such a wide variety of life and work in the County, from Customs and Traditions, Industry, the Countryside, with every aspect of farming, textiles, pottery, tourism, museums, the list was never ending. Everyone had been so willing to let us have details and histories of their particular trade. There was so much for the visitors to see and learn from the beautiful arrangements. One of the last items included was headed 'Villages in Change' was and still is worthy, of further consideration, the future of Rural Communities! In Castleton, thirty years ago, there were 860 on the Electoral Roll, in 2007 it stood at 536, ten years later? We were aware that this Festival would be more expensive to set up, with the large number of arrangements.

We all hoped this would bring unity and evangelism among our visitors, showing the love of Jesus, whatever creed or country we belong to. The visitors were very generous in showing their appreciation of the wonderful display and a magnificent sum was raised.

The CEFAA members had put a lot of effort into it, so it was agreed £100.00 would be divided between two charities of their choice, "Safe & Sound" a charity in Derby and "Unicef", £500.00 to St. Edmund's PCC, for use and facilities. The final total, including these amounts was £2,000.00, we had been able to cover our expenses. The remaining balance went to the Friends of St. Edmund's, who provide money for the structural maintenance of the church.

The Organic Garden weekend that year, raised over £500.00, which was amazing, with all the problems that we had encountered, but we were getting back to normal !

Thank goodness for our little caravan, we were able to have two weeks' holiday at Sandringham in July, when many areas were having floods and apart from an odd thunderstorm, we never required our raincoats!

In August, we heard there was going to be an 'Open Day' at the Dog's Trust in Leeds, so we went for

Sandringham Woods

Lavender garden in Norfolk

four nights to a club site at Boroughbridge, going to the open day on the way home. Cassie came from the Leeds centre and the manageress was at the entrance when we arrived, it was six years since we had been back, but she remembered Cassie's name! Oh what fun, there was an Agility course, just what Cassie enjoyed. She was one of the few dogs to complete the course off her lead, of course there was a round of applause, she then thought she should have two more goes, with Pat charging round the course, attempting to keep up with her!

To get us fully recuperated for the winter and as Muriel was due to have Radio Active Iodine the third week in November, we decided to go to Devon and the Cotswolds for two weeks in September, again we were lucky with the weather.

On the home front, we were still busy fundraising for church, a never ending task. The sound system had to be moved out of the back vestry, to make room for the toilet and the Font was moved to the Chancel, to allow room for a portable ramp into the back vestry, for disabled access, when the toilet was installed!

From Cross Street looking towards
Winnets Pass and the mountains

The bad news was, that the
boiler was condemned and its
replacement had to take
priority. Muriel, as PCC
secretary, was kept busy.
Meanwhile, Pat was also kept
busy, preparing for our stall at

A ride around the village

the Losehill Hall event, December 16th, which went very well and raised
£642.73. The previous year, after a similar event, had raised £509.26.
Most evenings, we were hand bell ringing, for Village Aid (Africa). We began
to wonder what else could happen?

On Christmas Eve, when Castleton is seething with visitors, we had a
crib service, hurrying up to church on a narrow road and much narrower
pavement, Pat got caught by the wing mirror of a Jeep, she was thrown to the
ground, but got up quickly and continued to church for the service, where
cold compresses were applied, no bones broken, but it took a lot of treatment

to get it better. Of course it doesn't help when you are walking through a field with the dog and find a sheep in trouble, which happened on two occasions, not a soul about, they are heavy with a full fleece and bloated abdomen, but somehow the good Lord gives you the strength to pull them over.

In Dickensian style, Gary roasts chesnuts during the Christmas period outside his traditional sweet shop

Muriel's thyroid treatment went well, although she had terrible chilblains, which she hadn't had since her late teens! Her legs were and still are, very discoloured, she also has Macular degeneration. Due to the blood vessels in her eyes being thin and wavy, the treatment suggested to treat the condition, was injections into the eyes, with a risk of going through a vessel leading to blindness. Muriel felt the risk was too great and it would be better to lose sight slowly rather than suddenly. Instead, she wears orange spectacles, to cut down the U/V rays and has a diet high in Lutin and extra Vitamin E and Zinc, hoping that the deterioration will be very slow.

From 2006 onwards, we held frequent produce stalls in church, when we made and sold homemade bread, cakes, quiches, biscuits, teacakes, Soup in the winter, marmalade, jam, lemon curd, chutney, you 'say it, we made it'

although we hasten to add, it was all suitable for vegetarians! This was sometimes monthly or fortnightly, at busy times, more frequently, continuing until we attempted to slow down, in May 2012. The amount made would vary, but we mainly took £200.00 to £350.00 on each produce stall. There

The extensive wooded areas near Oban

was also a bric-a-brac stall, manned by church friends. From 2006 to the beginning of May 2012, the produce we made and the bric-a-brac stalls, raised over £15,000.00, for church maintenance funds.

We did enjoy regular breaks in our little caravan, in April 2008 we went to Perth and Oban, although the weather was mixed, we had some lovely, forest walks, from the campsite just outside Oban, we took lots of pictures, Cassie loved every minute. Then in July, we had two weeks in Sandringham, from which we never tire. We continued to open our garden for two days in June, until 2015, usually raising at least £500.00 on each occasion.

Pat was the "Calamity Jane" on the 12th of August 2008! Our neighbour at that time had two dogs and she often worked 12 hour days. We would mind them, usually letting them in the garden, but on this occasion, we decided to go a bit farther afield, unfortunately, the young Rhodesian Ridgeback and another dog had previously taken a mutual dislike to each other two week's earlier and didn't we meet them again! Pat was twisted round and sent flying, landing hard on the ground with a fractured femur! Not very pleasant and hellishly painful! The surgeon was able to plate it and she soon showed she could get around on crutches and go up steps, therefore able to manage at home.

Muriel was busy with the Horticultural Section for Hope Show, on August Bank Holiday Monday there was a lot to do, so Pat was organised with a table, the telephone, entry forms, etc. becoming the "deputy secretary", answering phone calls of those wanting to enter some of the classes.

Even on the day, with some discomfort, managing to undertake, between 12.30pm and 3.30pm, the sorting out of the prize winners money into envelopes! Muriel arrived by car, to collect the prize envelopes, to give out at 4.00pm. So it was all very successful in the end, thanks to the steady flow of visitors all wanting to help. The elbow crutches played havoc with Pat's previous elbow injury, so she was pleased when she got down to one stick. Then becoming a regular visitor to the Chiropractor, who helped a lot. Cassie was very fed up with Pat walking slowly, but that soon improved.

We had earlier talked about having a Christmas Tree Festival inside church, to coincide with the village 'lights' switch on, when the shops and pubs decorate for the Christmas season the weekend after Remembrance Sunday. A decision was made to have a trial run of two weeks in November. Fortunately, the toilet and the kitchenette had been completed, a great improvement and well worth the cost of £15,500. The villagers were invited to place a Christmas tree, real or artificial, to advertise their organisation or their trade/business, to include a set of fairy lights. For the first year, we had 30 trees and provided refreshments for our visitors. The event was very successful and due to the hard work of all the helpers, we raised £1,639.03 for the church maintenance fund. We were always mindful that Advent is a penitential season, but there

Pat still on crutches. Cassie wonders why!

Cassie wins the Best Rescued Dog

was no objection from the church members, so for succeeding years, it was agreed, the festival would open daily from noon to 5.00pm for three weeks. We were happy to continue organising the event. At this time of the year, we should remember others, as well as ourselves, so we had two trees decorated to represent the charities with individual collecting tins.

To continue in 2010 with our other events.

The good news, we found an upholsterer to make cushions for the length of each pew in church! In that year, we joined the Caravan club, as well as the camping club, which gave us more options.

In April we had three weeks in the caravan, spending five nights at the Welwyn Garden site and we were able to visit friends in the vicinity.

Then we took the bull by the horns and ventured onto the M25, then the M4, going to Gowerton at the edge of the beautiful Gower peninsular. It

I do like to be beside the seaside!

brought back memories of when we took the youth group camping to Oxwich Bay in the 1960's, when it poured with rain. On this occasion we were lucky and apart from a few odd showers, we had a great time, including Cassie who was then 14 years old.

In July we went to Anglesey for two weeks, on the second week, we had a 70 miles an hour gale, which brought down an ash tree at the side of the site. We were alright, our caravan has a roof that pushes up, so we pulled it back down at midnight and we had already put the 'tie down' on the awning so we went to sleep. Apparently, half the campers were taking their awnings down at 1.00am in the pouring rain!

2011 was a fairly routine year, until the latter part, when we met Lee and Carl who had taken over the 'Three Roofs' Café. They were the owners of Pippin, a ten month old, wheaten terrier, Cassie was very friendly with her. They hadn't had her very long when they realised she was pregnant, the previous owner had a male wheaten terrier as well as other animals. Being under one year old, she would not be able to have her offspring registered. She would be due to give birth around Christmas time. Pat had a friend Barbara, who was an expert with dogs and she came and brought birthing equipment and gave lots of advice.

Seven puppies!

Just before Christmas, Pippin delivered seven puppies! She was an excellent mother, but the time came when homes had to be found for them and Pippin could enjoy what was left of her own puppy days. We often had Pippin, as there was no garden at the café and she enjoyed being in our garden.

In 2012 little Cassie died at the end of March on Good Friday, it was all very sudden, probably precipitated by cold weather. On the previous evening she didn't seem well. We stayed up with her, but in the middle of the night we had to take her to the vet, on the

Cassie dies at 16 years

Monty is rescued and starts winning rosettes

journey, she virtually died in Muriel's arms. She was almost 16 years old and although it was a shock, she'd had a good life, with no suffering. We arrived home at 4.00 am, when in our sorrow, we had to brace ourselves to take the Good Friday service that we had promised to undertake. So putting on a good face, we welcomed the parents and children to their special service at 10.00 am.

The house without a dog was terrible and although it is sad when they die, at least we are giving a rescue dog a good life. So the search began for another dog! We were not impressed by the large rescue centres, where the dogs seem so stressed, being behind glass with hordes of people staring at them. Eventually, we went to West Yorkshire Dog Rescue and the director Kathy is an angel. She takes all the dogs into her own home, until they have been vetted and any treatment required is given, then they are fostered, so they are not stressed, then Kathy advertises them on the Internet. On the 5th of May we adopted a Jack Russell dog, about nine years old. He was and still is a charmer!

He has a longer body than most JR's, with Queen Anne front legs and could trot along like anything. He had no name, so we chose Monty and he was a very quick learner! Monty was due to be castrated, which we organise with our vet. Petlog contacted us to have his scan details updated and they confirmed that he was born in 2001, so he was 11 years old! We later learned that Kathy had rescued Monty from a dog pound, where he was due to be put down.

Once again, in May, the weather was not good, this always seems to happen when it is nearing our special Garden Weekend in June. But one always has to make the best of it and on this occasion we raised over £500.00. We were fortunate at all these weekends to have our friend Margaret from Sheffield who came out to help us.

We then made plans to go away in July, Monty got very excited when we got the caravan out of the garage, our first stop was West Ayton, Scarborough, it was a lovely site with lots of rabbits. On the first night Monty thought he would join them and nipped under the awning, with Muriel going post-haste after him! It was mixed weather, alternate days had been fine, and we were able to go on the sands. Monty had his first introduction of going to church, he behaved perfectly. We stayed on the site for ten days, then journeyed to a small village, near Huntingdon. With the mixed weather, we were on a hard standing, rather than grass, but the rain still came under the awning. On the site there was a very nice restaurant and we invited friends

The good life with Muriel

On holiday in Norfolk

Monty likes to win, takes after Cassie

On the old rail track, Woodhall Spa

who lived fairly close, to come and spend a day with us and we all had a good meal there.

We had a short break of five nights at Blackshaw Moor caravan site, near Leek. We took Monty's girlfriend, Pippin, with us. It was a lovely site with plenty of long walks. Whilst there we went to a dog show at Sandbach, entering the dogs for the Irish brace, which is for two dissimilar dogs, they came third. Monty also came second for the best rescued dog. It was a very happy, enjoyable break with fine weather.

There was also activity at the barn which backs onto our private road, the existing owner claiming the grass verge on our road belonged to the barn! This was not true. The auctioneer knew this and assured us he was only selling the barn!

What a winter 2013 was, we had more snow than usual, although we quite enjoyed it when it was nice and crisp. Monty enjoyed it, even though his six inch legs had to leap through at least twelve inches of snow! Fortunately it didn't last long, but the mud it leaves behind is even worse. Then the 'up and over' garage door which housed the caravan needed attention. On looking through the 'Yellow Pages', we found a garage door repairer, who came out and found that it was beyond repair, so he made sure the door was secured and measured up for an automatic door. In the midst of all this, we decided to change the car. The new one arrived, when we were having gales. The car was put into the second garage, then the wind twisted the door, and one side was broken, there it was suspended with the new car in the garage! A quick telephone call to our friendly repairer and he said he would be with us within a short time. On arrival he had to gingerly hold the door whilst Pat got the car out. So we ended up with two automatic doors! They are great, just press the button and up they go – magic, press again and it comes down!

In April we had a Coffee morning for Christian Aid, whilst busy serving the coffee, Muriel noticed a lady sitting by herself at a table, so went to talk to her. She had for over 20 years worked in Africa, some time ago she was on her way to one of the Universities to see if she could obtain a teaching post, when her car became

Fun in the snow

Who will finish first?

Monty and Muriel looking at his prizes

firmly stuck in mud at some crossroads. A gentleman stopped to help her, she told him where she was going, he said please stop here, the people desperately need help. She was on the outskirts of Mali. Her name was Pam Young and we invited her to our home to tell us more about their plight. Pam had formed a little known Charity - Village Ventures (Africa), she lived in the Valley and three or four times a year she went by car to Mali, taking food and various other items, to try and help the people to be self sufficient. We both felt we would like to help her.

As a birthday present, Muriel started to have help in the garden, a local 'Jack of all trades' started coming two half days a month, from March to October, undertaking the more strenuous work.

His first job was to renew the wildlife pond, which was leaking. With a little help, the garden was ready to be opened for two days in June, when the

At the Woodhall site

weather was kind and we had a stall and light refreshments. We were delighted to raise £600.00 for our two new charities, West Yorkshire Dog Rescue and Pam's Village Ventures (Africa).

We were trying to do a little less, the first to go were the regular produce stalls in church. Then we gave advance notice that this would be our last year for organising the Christmas Tree Festival. Some of the members thought we should open the festival for four weeks, as the fourth week is the busiest in Castleton, after a degree of 'arm twisting' we agreed

On the old rail track

to do this. Lastly, we decided that this year, would be the last for us undertaking the Horticultural section at Hope Show, we had enjoyed doing it, but it was a very long, hard day from 7.30am to 5.30pm. We will look forward to future years, when we will be able to walk round and look at all the other stands and the judging of the animals.

It was good to get away in our caravan, starting with two weeks in April at Woodhall Spa, also taking Pippin with us, they enjoyed each other's company. There is always a commemorative dog show for the past instigator of the Cross Breed and Mongrel Club, which we liked to support. Also, if you have never been there, it is a delightful area, with a lot of history and a World War Two museum, a cinema in the wood, good restaurants and much more. In July we went to West Runton, Norfolk, a lovely site and only a mile from the sands. It was while there we visited the Hillside Animal Sanctuary, a short walk from the campsite, we were impressed by the amount of work being undertaken mainly by volunteers.

Muriel shows some of the flags from the camp sites we have visited. This is our little caravan

In September our dog club held their Annual meeting and dog show at Little Staughton, near Grafham Water, where there was a good Caravan Club site.

We stayed there for five nights, the dog show was only a short drive away. The Saturday was a fun day when Pedigrees and Mongrels can enter. Pippin was first in the Dog with the waggiest tail, Monty won one second and two fourth prizes. On the Sunday only mongrels could enter. Monty excelled himself by winning three First Prizes, the main one was the overall best rescued dog, as well as the rosette, he had a small trophy. He also won a first in the Super Veteran Class (dogs 11 years plus) three thirds and two in sixth place. It was a good day! We finished the season by going to Sandringham for almost a fortnight, as the weather forecast was good. With all the holidays in 2013, we never had wet raincoats, it may have rained during the night, but we had blue skies and sunshine! Our last Christmas Tree Festival was a great success, although the extra week, followed by Christmas, left us very happy with the result, but tired!

Muriel and Monty on the beach

It was a relief at the start of 2014, mainly because we had relinquished two major events! But we were still busy!

Muriel was not able to drive now due to her macular degeneration, but Pat had passed her DVLA eye test for a further three years. So we had been for our usual break to Woodall Spa in April, both of us in fine shape! Then, on May 15th, we were having a Coffee Morning for Christian Aid, to be held in the Chapel. We had taken Monty for a walk, collecting the newspaper, on the way back, Pat tripped over a curb and fell full length on her nose, mouth, neck, rib cage and her right hand. She looked a mess! Fortunately, she had an appointment within a couple days with a physiotherapist, but it took over three months to really improve.

Camping at Wagtail Country Park 2016

At the end of May, we had such strong winds, our lovely white lilac was blown down, fortunately, a tree surgeon in the village got it upright and firmly stabilized, so we hope it will recover. It was a bit hard having the garden open in June, but it had been advertised, so it was a case of "where there's a will there's a way". In the end it all went well. We revisited the West Runton site in July for two weeks, Pat had a problem knocking in the tent pegs for the awning with her left hand, but we managed between us!

We also made a return visit to Little Staughton, but this time we camped with the other club members on the campsite. It was an enormous field and we had a lazy time, with no dashing hither and thither.

We were unable to go away in October as Pat was booked to have a cataract operation at Claremont, which was very successful. Our good friend Carl insisted he was taking me, waiting until it was all over to bring me home.

The first book launch in February 2017

We still have plenty to keep us busy, as well as Monty and often Pippin to care for, at the same time the trials of old age are just around the corner, as we are slowing down.

We have had an amazing journey, from 1966 to 2014, which is now coming to an end. At times, we have had to remember the saying we have used in the book, "Think big and your deeds will grow, Think small and you will fall behind, Think that you can and you will!"

Those who have read our first book, will remember our promise made in 1946, we hope you will agree that we have fulfilled that.

Yes, Life is what YOU make it!

The Prologue

Having ended our second and final book in 2014, we now wish to reflect on and consider the special events which occurred in 2015 to 2017, when our first book was launched.

To reflect: we have been blessed with energy and willpower to enjoy our hectic lives. We hope you will agree, we have given of our time and talents, to help others less fortunate than ourselves. At the same time, we have been able to visit most areas of our beautiful Great Britain, before much has been spoiled by what some might call progress! Living at a slower pace, with time to appreciate the world around us, has changed.

Not for us, talking on mobiles non-stop night and day, nor headphones, with the latest tunes, to the oblivion of those around us. We benefited from our camping, later trailer tenting, followed by having a small caravan, then canal holidays. It was rewarding to see the cadets we took camping, blossom year by year into leaders of their Section, a training which would help them in the future.

Following our Mother's insistence that we should always save by investing in policies, when they matured, we could buy or do something special, which is how we purchased our caravan and five weeks in Canada and America.

We took pride in our homes, both in Sheffield and Castleton, Muriel as the gardener, with green fingers, also the washer up! Pat the 'labourer' and cook. We have been privileged to welcome hundreds of visitors into our garden and home, who have helped by supporting our money-making events, in particular, we are indebted to our friends and neighbours for their help.

Christianity has been our rock, although at times seriously tested, but our faith is now as strong as ever. We are awaiting a change in the Valley, will it be a male or maybe a female to lead us in our journey?

In 2015 and 2016, we have continued raising money in our traditional ways, although on Shrove Tuesday in 2015, we invited ten locals for a three course vegetarian lunch (£10), which was very enjoyable and raised money for our two charities.

We learned a lot editing the Parish Magazine, and in our tenth year, we

Receiving our Certificate of Achievement at Westminster Central Hall from Rev. Tony Miles

noticed details of a competition organised by the Association of Magazine Editors in the Diocesan News and we decided to have a go!

What a lovely surprise, when we learned that although we had not won the top prize, we were being awarded a framed Certificate of Achievement, with an invitation to their Annual Meeting and presentation of the awards at the Westminster Central Hall, London, May 2016. Our friend Carl who was going to London that day, offered to take us, along with his young nephew. After an early start, we arrived at the Hall at 10.00am, after an excellent day, our 'chauffer' came at 3.30pm for our journey home. Monty, our dog, was looked after by our friend Lee and his dog Pippin. After ten years, this award was the 'icing on the cake' for us.

Later that year, with Muriel's Macular degeneration, making it increasingly difficult to proofread, we felt the time had come to retire from editing the magazine.

Monty with two rosettes won in April 2017

We wrote a piece in the December magazine asking for a new editor? Yes, we do believe in Angels, we meet them frequently! Ruth, a newcomer to the village, agreed to take over in March 2017, and with her expertise, she is doing a fantastic job, Muriel and I are eternally grateful.

Before we leave 2016, our neighbours in Millbridge celebrated the Queen's 90th Birthday with us.

In February 2017, we had the excitement of launching our first book, which after three months, became a best seller and we had to order a reprint! So far with the generosity of so many, since the launch, we have raised well over £4,500. Which has been divided between our two Charities. Our grateful thanks to everyone.

The two Charities we support, have no 'middle man', every penny goes to where it is needed. Wendy at Hillside Animal Sanctuary, does amazing work, investigating cases of cruelty and giving a home to so many beautiful

Monty and Pippin wishing a Happy Christmas

animals, who have suffered so much. Pam is currently in Mali, preparing for 250 cataract operations in December, gathering the medical equipment that is required. She now has a telephone, ringing us on September 18th to let us know she was well.

For our readers, you should realize that she is in her late 60's and travels by car (the cheapest way) to Mali, living with them, on this particular journey for four months. She has been working in this area for over ten years, during which time she has provided and supported these poorest of people with goods, teaching them how to become self-sufficient and they now have classrooms and equipment for the children. One woman, doing what she has done, is worthy of the highest recommendation.

In closing our prologue, may we hope for the future benefit of Great Britain, that our leaders begin to realize that common sense must become the 'In word' in the future. We must do away with the horrid common purpose, which has led to bullying and treating everyone the same!

Everyone is unique, no two people are alike and should be dealt with accordingly. To treat everyone the same will lead to stress and depression.

We hope you have enjoyed our books,

Muriel and Patricia Callis.

THE UNIVERSITY
OF BIRMINGHAM
WESTHILL

Muriel Callis

···

has completed the course

in

EDUCATION FOR MINISTRY

July, 2001

··························· UK Director for
EFM

··························· Principal/Pro Vice
Chancellor

THE UNIVERSITY
OF BIRMINGHAM
WESTHILL

Patricia Callis

....

has completed the course

in

EDUCATION FOR MINISTRY

July, 2001

.... UK Director for
EFM

.... Principal/Pro Vice
Chancellor

The Star
WOMEN'S WALK

TheStar
WALK

This is to certify that

Patricia M. Callis

was placed _____ 13th _____

the Womens Race of nine miles on
Tuesday June 1st. 1982 recording a time of
___ 1 ___ hours ___ 51 ___ minutes ___ 47 ___ seconds

Under AAA rules and regulations

Editor, The Star

~ notes ~

~ notes ~